W9-BYS-993

MINIMUM DISCLOSURE

MINIMUM DISCLOSURE

How the Pentagon
Manipulates the News

Juergen Arthur Heise

W.W. Norton & Company

NEW YORK

Copyright © 1979 by W. W. Norton & Company, Inc.
Published simultaneously in Canada by George J. McLeod Limited,
Toronto. Printed in the United States of America.

All Rights Reserved

First Edition

Library of Congress Cataloging in Publication Data

Heise, Juergen Arthur.
    Minimum disclosure.

    Includes bibliographical references and index.
    1. The military and the press—United States.
2. Government information—United States
3. Freedom of information—United States. 4. United
States. Dept. of Defense. I. Title.
PN4745.H4 1979   070.4'3   78–24580
ISBN 0–393–05696–1

This book is typeset in Times Roman
Manufactured by the Haddon Craftsmen
Design by Jacques Chazaud

1 2 3 4 5 6 7 8 9 0

To the most valiant person
I have ever known,
my late mother

Contents

~~~~~~~~~~~~~~~~~~~~~~~~~~~~~~

Introduction

A series of sporadic and sometimes puzzling incidents provided the original impetus for this book. They occurred in the late 1960s and early 1970s when I worked as a newspaper reporter and a freelancer. At the U.S. Military Academy, for example, access to cadet barracks was denied, particularly during the hours when senior cadets disciplined erring newcomers. In contrast, the Naval Academy allowed visits to similar facilities without hesitation.

More puzzling still, one three-starred superintendent of the U.S. Air Force Academy would supply a range of requested documents without delay, but his successor would rule that such material was for internal use only and need not be released. More important, whereas the former would permit interviews with any cadet, faculty member, or administrator who wished to talk, the latter flatly barred such interviews, a prohibition that stayed in force until publicity and congressional interest in the case caused it to be lifted.

The Freedom of Information Act was of course on the books in those days, but information officers and their commanders were often unfamiliar with its content. When it was called to their attention, the not infrequent response ran along these lines: "Why do you want to look into these things anyway? We're doing a good job. Why don't you write about that? After all, we're on the same side—aren't we?"

My experiences were, of course, not unusual. Others working for the media ran into the same problem but on a larger scale, particularly in connection with the war in Vietnam. The daily press briefings by the American command in Saigon became known as the "five o'clock follies." The phrase "credibility gap" was coined. Two of the most prestigious American newspapers were temporarily enjoined from printing the Pentagon's official history of the involvement in Vietnam. And on and on.

The phenomenon could, of course, always be explained in broad political terms. For various reasons, the executive branch over the years had gained greater and greater power. To keep and expand these powers, it sought to exercise ever-increasing control over information in its possession. That way, it could deprive critics of ammunition and shore up support for favored policies and programs through the selective release of bits of information at the appropriate moment. But that explanation also implies that effective, central control can be exercised over a very large, very complex, very farflung bureaucracy.

Such control may be possible, at least for a time, over issues at the macropolitical level. But what about scenarios being played out on lower political levels? Can such central control be exercised effectively at those levels also? Or is it possible that other, less sweeping factors are at play? For instance, is it possible that the phenomenon, particularly below the macropolitical level, could be the result, at least in part, of the way modern formal organizations and their members behave?

Fascination with the phenomenon and a continuing interest in the American military as an organization spurred on my search for answers to two essential questions: How does the Department of Defense handle newsworthy information that is negative in nature—at least from the Pentagon's perspective— but that it legally has no right to withhold? Why is such information treated as it is?

A search of the literature on the subject shed only a sliver of light on these questions. Thus, I decided to explore the issue. This book is the culmination of that exploration. It takes a long, hard look at a much-ignored aspect of the government-media relationship. To make that look as penetrating as possible, some of the skills of the investigative reporter were used to dig up information. To keep it from being little more than an interesting anecdote riddled by the usual problems of *ex post facto* research, some of the techniques of the social scientist were harnessed.

Building on the work of others, I identified a number of plausible but competing factors, all, some, or none of which might provide a clue to what motivates the Pentagon to treat "bad" news the way it does. To get a more valid fix on these variables, more than one method was used to collect information about each. In-depth interviewing, involving five dozen individuals, was used extensively. (Names are named unless anonymity was requested for part or all of an interview. The ranks and titles given are as of 1974–75 when most of the field research was conducted.) As much or more information came from current and archival files, testimony given before Congress and in legal proceedings, personal documents, informants, and the usual literature search.

What I found is, I hope, far from the last word on the subject. The time has come—indeed, is long overdue—for an intensive examination of the public information mechanisms employed not only by the Pentagon but by government generally, whether in Washington, D.C., or in Spokane, Washington. The country is clearly looking for much more open government, yet the research for this book showed that the prevailing attitude within the bureaucracy is to conduct the business of public information as usual.

No matter how firmly we close our eyes, however, an array of questions will keep begging for sound answers. For instance, can we continue to blithely tolerate that all-too-pervasive notion that somehow government officials can keep the lid on information that runs counter to a pet project or that undermines a favorite policy? Can we continue to accept that public information is not a respectable career field, that it is a sanctuary for a political friend owed a soft spot or for an ex-reporter who wants to come in from the cold?

More fundamentally, has the time come to break with the corporate public relations model? Do we need to develop a model for the public sector based on the premise that the mobilization and retention of long-term public support is possible only through the release of the maximum amount of information with a minimum of delay, distortion, or obfuscation? Given the American political context, can a workable public information program be built around the idea that candor is vital in fair and foul situations alike, so vital that releasable information will be forthcoming even if its publication at times may cause great pain.

And these questions must not only be asked of the Defense Department. My experiences during 1976–77 as a postdoctoral public administration faculty fellow assigned to the assistant secretary for public affairs at the Department of Health, Education, and Welfare made that painfully clear. That year underlined that no department has a monopoly on inept public information operations. For example, HEW has its share of competent professionals among the careerists working in its public information offices, but it still has far too many who see their job primarily in terms akin to those held dear by the PR man for Snake Oil, Inc.

Compounding the problem is the quality of the political appointees who are brought in to oversee HEW's public information activities. It is not difficult, for instance, to find among them once highly esteemed journalists who are almost completely unqualified as administrators—a distinct handicap for someone suddenly in charge of scores of employees and a budget of millions. Such ex-reporters, however, are among the better appointees—at least they know something about the media. Others also know next to nothing about management, but even less about American journalism. But they, too, have good political connections.

This study took me down a path—and into various cul-de-sacs—longer, rockier, and more twisting than originally anticipated. Only the gracious support of a number of persons made it possible to get down that path however far I did.

I am deeply indebted to a very busy Alan K. Campbell for suffering through all too many pages of the original "draft." I owe a similar debt to Guthrie Birkhead, James D. Carroll, John C. Honey, Henry F. Schulte, and Dwight Waldo.

My editors at W.W. Norton and Company were superb. I will always be grateful to Eric P. Swenson for the stimulating exchange of ideas he initiated and to Sharon Morgan for wielding a very sharp pencil so intelligently.

Once more, I am also deeply indebted to Carey McWilliams, until recently with *The Nation,* who, as always, acted when others talked.

I thank the Louis M. Rabinowitz Foundation of New York for helping defray some of the costs of the field research.

To Margaret Wickline and Evelyn Medina I apologize for submitting their eyesight to unnecessary strain as they typed and retyped the manuscript. I thank both for their diligence and skill.

I owe the greatest debt to my wife and son, Simine and Mark. Their patience and understanding are miracles I will never fully comprehend. And only the never-faltering encouragement of the "Patient Persian" kept various drafts and several boxes of documents from further polluting Biscayne Bay and the Potomac River.

MINIMUM DISCLOSURE

1

A Case in Point: Squelching the My Lai Massacre

It had been a hectic winter for Lt. General William R. Peers, and the pace became quicker still as spring approached. The three-star general had been very busy ever since the secretary of the army and its chief of staff appointed him in November 1969 to head an official inquiry to determine what had happened at My Lai 4 in South Vietnam a year and a half earlier. More specifically, he was ordered to find out how adequate the original investigation had been of the March 16, 1968 events at My Lai, and whether anyone had suppressed or withheld information about the incident.

According to a front-page story in the New York *Times* of the next morning, a successful battle had been fought at My Lai that day. A two-column headline in the middle of the page—atop a story attributed to the "American headquarters" in Saigon—proclaimed, "G.I.'s, in Pincer Move, Kill 128 in Daylong Battle."

In the fall of the next year, a related story ran in the *Times*. It, however, was not a glowing description of a successful battle. Carrying the Associated Press logo and a Fort Benning, Georgia, dateline, it was tucked between the ads on page 14 of

the September 7, 1969 issue and ran for a total of 25 lines under
a minuscule headline: "Army Accuses Lieutenant in Vietnam
Deaths."

The AP story was based on a three-paragraph news release
that merely announced that the military was retaining on active
duty one Lt. William Calley because he was charged with having violated "Article 118 [of the Uniform Code of Military
Justice], murder, for offenses allegedly committed against civilians while serving in Vietnam in March 1968." Issued neither
by an "American headquarters" nor the Pentagon public affairs
office but by an army fort in the Deep South, the release did not
mention that the lieutenant faced six counts of murder or that
he stood accused of having deliberately shot 109 civilians.[1]

Only the diligence of a freelance investigative reporter and the
conscience of a concerned G.I. eventually revealed that what
was originally heralded as a successful battle was in reality a
massacre of scores of Vietnamese civilians.

These revelations made the winter of 1969–70 a busy one for
General Peers. Then 56 years old, the general, who had himself
spent 30 months in Vietnam as a troop commander, moved
swiftly to get the inquiry under way. He assembled a staff that
would eventually number 86, including a "distinguished jurist
of impeccable integrity" whom Peers asked to have as his legal
counsel to guard against civilian criticism about the inquiry's
objectivity and impartiality.[2]

Within a week of Peers's appointment, the panel was working
six days a week taking testimony from witnesses in a Pentagon
basement room. In the meantime, a special liaison office was set
up in Saigon to help collect information in Vietnam. Late in
December, Peers himself and several members of his staff went
there for ten days. They questioned witnesses—military as well
as civilian, American and Vietnamese—inspected parts of Son
My Village, of which My Lai 4 was a part, on foot, and swept
over other areas with a helicopter.

With Peers in Southeast Asia, his deputy, a civilian lawyer
from the army's general counsel's office, continued to interro-
gate witnesses at the Pentagon. Eventually, three interrogation

teams worked simultaneously to speed up the inquiry. That way 399 witnesses would be questioned, several repeatedly. Concurrently, the evidence and transcribed testimony were reviewed and edited, amounting by early March 1970 to thousands of pages, divided into four volumes: a report of the inquiry's findings and recommendations; the verbatim testimony of witnesses and summaries of their testimony; other evidence; and statements made to the army's Criminal Investigation Division.

By the middle of March 1970, the whole effort reached its climax. A special team of army lawyers was going over the evidence to determine whether it was sufficient; the statute of limitations would run out on March 16 in the cases of individuals accused of covering up what had happened at My Lai. Meanwhile, Peers had a three-hour meeting with the assistant secretary of defense for public affairs to be prepped for a news conference to be held on March 17.[3]

At that conference, Peers told reporters that the "inquiry clearly established that a tragedy of major proportions occurred there [in Son My Village] on that day." He also announced that charges had been filed against 14 officers, ranging from failure to obey regulations to dereliction of duty to false swearing in connection with what had occurred at Son My two years earlier.

The press focused on the accusations against the commanding general of the Americal Division, some of whose units were responsible. He had since been appointed to the prestigious superintendency of West Point. Moreover, he, along with his deputy at the Americal, were the first two generals facing a possible court-martial in 18 years.

But one of the reporters did ask the general whether there was any evidence that the behavior reflected in the charges was "more widespread than what had happened at My Lai on March 16." Had it happened in other places or on other days? Replied Peers: "If there is, I have no knowledge of it. It was not brought out to me in the evidence. . . ."

Next question: "What about the Son My area on that day?" The journalist pointed out that some of the charges made were placed against an officer of the Americal Division company operating not at My Lai 4 that day but at My Khe, another hamlet within Son My village, more than a mile from the site of the My Lai 4 incident.

Instead of dealing with the charges against the officer from B Company and the circumstances surrounding them, the general explained the confusion involving the geographical nomenclature of Son My village and My Lai 4, pointing out that the latter was a subvillage of the former and that, when his panel discovered that fact, it was decided to "refer to it as Son My village rather than try to delineate it to that one piece of terrain, My Lai 4."[4]

And that is where the reporters left it.

They were, of course, handicapped by the army's decision to release initially only about one-fifth of the 260-page first volume of the Peers inquiry. The part that was originally made public did not include the following paragraph:

> It is anticipated that only ten men in [B Company] directly participated in the killings and destruction in My Khe (4); two of these are dead and the remaining eight have either refused to testify or claim no recollection of the event. As a result, it has not been possible to reconstruct the events with certainty. *It appears, however, that the number of non-combatants killed by [B Company] on 16 March 1968 may have been as high as 90. The company reported a total of 38 [Viet Cong killed in action] on 16 March, but it is likely that few if any were Viet Cong.*[5] [emphasis added]

Seymour Hersh, who had earlier brought the My Lai massacre to light, managed while still working as a freelance writer to obtain copies of the Peers inquiry materials. They formed the basis for articles that appeared in *The New Yorker* and for a book in which he disclosed the killings of civilians at My Khe 4 that occurred on the same day as the incident at My Lai 4, and the cover-up, as he termed it, of the My Khe 4 situation and other matters.[6]

The army, nevertheless, refused to release most of the Peers inquiry material. At first it based the refusal on the Freedom of Information Act (FoIA) exemptions which permit the withholding of interoffice memoranda, of investigatory material prepared for law enforcement purposes, and of material whose release may constitute an invasion of privacy, and on the further position that the release might jeopardize the legal appeals of Lieutenant Calley. When the legal cases arising out of My Lai had been concluded, the army invoked a new reason: "national security." Various appeals, including one to the courts by a congressman, were unsuccessful, with the secretary of the army stating he would wait on the matter until Calley's case had been reviewed by the president.[7]

Finally, late in 1974, the secretary announced the release of volumes 1 and 3 of the inquiry. The other two were released in March 1975, with names and other information that might identify an individual removed to protect those not previously named.

However, during the field research for this study, I obtained access to a totally unsanitized version of volume 2 of the Peers inquiry. Amid the thousands of pages of transcripts of witness testimony, that of eight Americal Division information specialists was found, ranging from that of the army's own photographer-writer team on the scene at My Lai during the day of the massacre to the division's top information officer.

Although the handling of the information about the My Lai incident may not be typical of the way military public affairs specialists deal with "bad" news, the testimony and related information provide some unusually penetrating insights into the process.

The incident not only illustrates in rare, concrete—albeit, sometimes repulsive—detail *how* a large, complex public organization treats negative information it knows to be of interest to the media; it also provides some clues as to *why* such "blackeye stories" are handled as they are.

The My Lai Incident and the Role
of Public Information Specialists

Specialist Fifth Class Jay A. Roberts and Sergeant Ronald L. Haeberle were on the second wave of helicopters that lifted elements of the Americal Division to a landing zone near My Lai 4 shortly after 7:30 A.M. on March 16, 1968. The combat troops they were accompanying were part of Task Force Barker, which, in turn, was made up of various troops of the 11th Brigade of the Americal Division. Roberts was a combat correspondent with the 31st Information Detachment of the 11th Brigade and Haeberle a photographer.

Haeberle, trained in photography as an undergraduate, carried two types of cameras. One belonged to the army and used black and white film that could be developed by the information detachment; the other, his own, contained his color film, which could not be developed in the field. He would process it himself after having left the army.

Both men remained with C Company as it approached My Lai 4 and then swept through the village. The troops encountered no resistance during the approach nor the sweep of the village, but "killed at least 175–200 Vietnamese men, women and children," including "only 3 or 4 [who] were confirmed as Viet Cong." The inhabitants were killed either individually as the troops moved through the village or rounded up in groups. One of the groups consisted of 70 to 80 persons who were taken to a ditch east of the village and later shot there; another group of 20 to 50 persons was shot on a trail south of the hamlet; a smaller group "of 7–12 women and children" was simply "rounded up and killed." In addition, the army's official investigation found that several women were raped, houses were burned, and livestock killed. C Company suffered exactly one casualty: "One man from the company was reported as wounded from the accidental discharge of his weapon."[8]

Haeberle and Roberts, there to record the action for the brigade information office, saw much of this activity. Roberts, for example, told the Peers inquiry of the following incident,

seen as one group of soldiers moving through My Lai 4 brought
a group of women and children out of a "hootch":

> They grabbed one of the girls and started to tear her blouse
> off, as I can remember, and an old lady who, I guess, was her
> mother or related, was biting and kicking and scratching and
> fighting off all these G.I.'s that were harassing this girl. Ha-
> eberle went to take a picture of this thing, and they spotted
> him and his camera, and everybody froze and turned their
> backs and said, "Watch it. He's got a camera!" They stopped
> what they were doing, and they all turned away, and Haeberle
> took a picture of the group of people. There was some discus-
> sion as to what they were going to do with them, and some-
> body said, "Kill them." I started to walk away from them,
> because I didn't particularly want to see this. Anyhow, there
> was a lot of firing. One G.I. had an M-60. I don't know if they
> used that. There was some automatic fire. I don't recall
> whether it was the M-60 or an M-16. I'm not sure, but any-
> way I went on and turned around. I think Haeberle stayed
> behind for a little while. I know we got separated there for a
> minute or so.[9]

Haeberle and Roberts kept moving on. According to Roberts,
they next came upon "a pile of bodies" of men, women, and
children south of the village, spread over 15 to 20 feet along a
road and about 45 yards from where Roberts was. In his words:

> I didn't go out there. The first thing that happened with that
> group was there was a small child—a toddler, maybe 2 or 3
> years old—young. It was right in the area of these bodies and
> seemed to be searching or walking around, and a G.I. came
> along and saw him out there—saw that we were watching—
> dropped to one knee, got a good steady position with his
> M-16, and fired off a single shot and dropped the child, and
> I don't recall being revolted by it. I guess because of the
> distance, but it just seemed awfully strange. Probably any
> number of things ran through my mind, but I just recall this
> happening, and it was after this that Haeberle walked out
> there and took a picture.

They kept moving. Sometime later they came upon this scene, described in nearly identical terms by both Roberts and Haeberle. In the photographer's words:

A small child came walking toward me and he needed medical attention, and he was shot through the arm and shot through the foot around the ankle. And, he kept walking toward me, and I kept on focusing, and I kept backing up and backing up. This G.I. knelt down beside me. I didn't know it at the time, because I kept taking the camera and backing up. Three shots were fired. The first shot hit him in the stomach. The second shot lifted him up in the air. The third shot put him down . . . a stroboscopic effect, one, two, three. And the body fluids came out of his back.

Both Roberts and Haeberle went on to describe other atrocities they saw that day. Haeberle estimated—emphasizing that his was "a rough estimate"—that he "saw probably about 20 people killed and about 50 people, altogether, dead. . . ."

By about 11:00 A.M., he and Haeberle left C Company. Roberts said that he "was looking for a story of American heroics in combat, and it appeared to me that any live fire fights, any possible action that would have taken place would have already in fact have taken place, and there was nothing there, now, but cleaning-up operations."

So the writer-photographer team boarded a helicopter that took them to a nearby area where another company was operating. They stayed there for about two hours, then caught another ride to the task force headquarters. Here Roberts said he interviewed the commander of Task Force Barker, some of whose troops had made the sweep through My Lai 4:

I just asked him for a statement, "Give me a quote on your opinion of the operation," things like that, and he said something to the effect that it had been highly successful. . . . And I asked him, of course—I seem to recall asking him about the high body count and the low number of weapons and he just indicated to me—you know—that I would do a good job writing the story, and said: "Don't worry about it," or something to that effect. He seemed to be happy with the way the operation had gone—that there was no polarization about the number of bodies, and I didn't ask him about the women and children at the time.

Putting It on Paper

Once the interview with the commander was completed, Haeberle and Roberts returned to the information office. The testimony of the various witnesses from the American Division's information specialists is unclear on who then wrote what for public release.

But it is clear that the information released bore little resemblance to what Roberts and Haeberle had seen. For example, the Americal News Sheet, dated one day after the massacre at My Lai—which was "published daily under the supervision of the [information officer], Americal Division"—carried a long story, starting on its first page, about the exploits of Task Force Barker at Son My. It pointed out in the first paragraph that the "128 enemy dead was the largest enemy body count reported by the 11th Brigade for a 24-hour period since they took control of Operation Muscatine." Not until the fourth paragraph did the story note that only three weapons were captured.[10]

The in-house publication of the 11th Infantry Brigade, *Trident,* carried an almost identical story in its March 22 issue. It, too, pointed to the 128 "enemy" killed and the three weapons captured.[11] Similar information was contained in an undated news release issued by the information office of the 11th Infantry Brigade under the byline of "SP5 Jay A. Roberts."[12]

More important, a "communiqué" issued on the day of the My Lai incident by the U.S. Military Assistance Command in Saigon announced to the world, "Americal Division forces have killed 128 enemy near Quang Ngai City." It, however, made no mention of the three weapons.[13]

In stark contrast, Radio Hanoi, in an English-language

broadcast in mid-April 1968, reported that the National Liberation Front (NLF) Committee in Quang Ngai Province—where
Son My village is located—issued a communiqué charging that
on March 16 of that year more than 500 people had been killed
in a "massacre" by the "U.S. imperialists [and] their hench-
men."[14]

Although riddled by its own propaganda and identifying
the wrong American military units as being responsible for
the action, the NLF account was closer to the testimony of
Roberts and Haeberle than was the material issued for public
release by the American military. Moreover, the NLF communiqué figure of 500 killed came close to the subsequent estimates of the Peers inquiry, which held that "the number of
Vietnamese killed in the overall area of Son My village may
have exceeded 400."[15]

While the Americal information specialists' testimony before
the inquiry does not make clear who wrote the material that was
to be released publicly, it does indicate why it was handled as
it was. The following exchange between the Peers panel and
Roberts provides some clarification:

Q. *You indicated that you had some concern in writing this
article which you prepared, evidently for the division newspaper?*

A. More or less, yes, sir. On each operation, we wrote a
release and sent it through channels to be cleared. When
it came back, we sent it to the reporter and advisors for
the paper in Saigon, and sent them to the home town of
any individual that starred in the action, and I did—I was
concerned with it—with how I was going to write an
article that made us sound like that we had carried out—
what sounded like it was the biggest operation in Vietnam
that day. It was the largest number of enemy killed that
day and drew quite a bit of attention, I guess, in the press
briefings the next day. I wrote it from the point of view
that it was successful because we had killed a large number
of VC.

Q. *Did you have any revulsion in writing such an article?*
A. I did when I first got back, I think. I seem to remember mentioning it to Lieutenant [Arthur J.] Dunn [11th Brigade press officer]. "How can I say this, that we killed all these people and didn't capture anything? It makes us look pretty bad." And he said, "Go ahead and write something. I'll help you with it," or something like that. When I wrote it, I more or less followed the lines that he had used when he made up his report to division, which mostly was just fact.

Q. *Had you discussed the civilians, women and children that were being killed, and all the facts you had observed with Lieutenant Dunn or Lieutenant Moody?*
A. I'm certain that I mentioned it to Lieutenant Dunn, but I don't recall mentioning it to Lieutenant [John W.] Moody [11th Brigade public information officer].

Ronald Haeberle, the photographer, had similar, although less specific, recollections of what happened when he and Roberts returned from My Lai 4 to the information office. Asked by the panel whether he reported what he had seen and photographed to his sergeant in the information office, he said, "I told them what I believe it was—I can't say it word for word, but it was mentioned, that I said something had happened. I believe there was women and children in this also, I believe I did mention that. But actually going and describing in detail every move, no."

Fellow enlisted man James E. Ford, a clerk in the information office, largely corroborated what Haeberle and Roberts said. He was asked what the writer and photographer said to him when they returned to the office:

A. Well, it wasn't just me. They came back to the office, I don't remember whether it was that same day or the next day, and said there had been a pretty big operation. They had gone to this village and wiped it out. That's about what they said.

Q. *Was that all they said?*
A. Yes, there—

Q. [*Interposing*] *Anybody ask what did they mean by wiping it out?*
A. Oh, we asked and they said, "We killed everything in the village."

Q. *Did anybody ask what that meant?*
A. No, sir. I think we understood what that meant.

Q. *What did it mean?*
A. That they'd killed everything in the village.

Q. *Such as?*
A. Such as all of the people that were in the village, men, women and kids.

In response to other questions, Ford also acknowledged that the figure of 128 enemy killed had been the highest he could recall being reported in connection with any battle up to that point, and that at no other time were there reports that an entire village had been "wiped out." Were the brigade information officer, Moody, and the press officer, Dunn, around when Haeberle and Roberts were recounting their experiences? Replied Ford: "I believe so, sir. It was in the office and it was during working hours, so I imagine they were there." But Ford also stated that Haeberle and Roberts were not outwardly upset about what they had seen:

Q. *They didn't come back and make some comment, "Boy, you should have seen them shooting," and all this sort of thing? They didn't have any great war stories to tell about all this?*
A. No, there wasn't anything emotional about it. As I said before, they went in and wiped out the village and that was it. There wasn't anything emotional.

Nor did he recall that either said that they had pictures of what had occurred. Indeed, Ford concluded his testimony by telling the Peers panel that, looking back now, if the activities at Son My village had been presented "a little bit more color-fully, with a little bit more detail and at a bit more length, well, I for one, think there would've been something said about it."

The senior noncommissioned officer of the 11th Brigade in-formation office, Sergeant John Stonich, who selected Haeberle and Roberts for the My Lai assignment because they "were my two senior people" and "seemed to be best qualified," did not recall that either the photographer or the writer were upset when they returned.

He was asked whether he was sure they "didn't tell you something about the unnecessary killing of women and children out there?" "Very positive, sir," he replied. Did he hear about it from any other sources? "In the office there was never a word uttered that you could hear about this operation," he said. But the sergeant did allow that he saw some of the black and white pictures that Haeberle had taken at My Lai 4.* He saw only some of those after they had been developed in the brigade's photo facilities and, then, "just in passing through." He recalled "one picture of an individual with a torch to a hut which I specifically said we would not enlarge, because it was not in keeping with standards, showing them burning a hut."

The next person in the chain of command above Haeberle and Roberts was the 11th Brigade press officer, Lieutenant Dunn. He recalled that he wondered at the time about the "vast dis-crepancy," as he termed it, between the 128 enemy reported

---

*The color photographs Haeberle took, using his own film and equipment, were not developed until after he left Vietnam. Some of these eventually appeared in *Life* magazine, many showing gruesome scenes. Of all the Haeberle pictures examined by the Peers panel, the black and white photos were "comparatively bland." As one member of the panel told Haeberle, "Practically without exception, all of the pictures of what might be termed atrocities appear in your color photos."

killed and the three weapons captured. He was asked whether
Haeberle and Roberts reported to him on the evening of March
16 on what they had done at My Lai 4. His response:

> Very little, as I recall . . . there was no need for them to report
> . . . although I do recall Sergeant Haeberle saying he got some
> good pictures. I don't know whether I personally asked him
> how it was out there, or whether somebody in the office asked
> them and then they told me about it. But in the back of my
> mind, I kind of recall that they didn't want to talk about it
> too much. This is pretty vague in my mind, but this is how
> —the way I recall it. And I don't know whether they talked
> to anybody else or not . . . but to my own knowledge, they
> didn't say much at all. I just got the impression that what they
> saw for some reason or other, they didn't want to talk about
> at any great length. This is not uncommon. I don't know
> whether they had ever seen—I know they had never seen an
> operation this big before, and I didn't know, maybe this was
> the first time they had seen dead bodies, enemy soldiers killed,
> or Americans wounded or, if there had been any Americans
> wounded, possibly this a—it might have affected them that
> way.

Dunn, when asked about the article that appeared in the 11th
Brigade *Trident,* acknowledged that he had written the first two
paragraphs on the night of March 16. Did he recall any discussions with Roberts about the preparation of the article? "No.
None, other than the fact that he seemed to be having trouble
writing a lead for it. So we finally decided to use the lead that
I had sent to division that night, the night of the 16th."

When some of the testimony by Roberts—involving the trouble he had writing the article because of what he had seen that
day and his discussion of the killing of women and children with
the press officer—was read to Dunn, he replied:

> I don't recall it, but as I say, I can't rule it out. It was a long
> time ago. I don't rule out the fact that he did talk to me about
> it. I have no—I just do not recall him mentioning anything

other than the fact that he could not write the lead and, well, I think he couldn't write the lead because I think he thought, or maybe knew, that the figures were—didn't quite jibe. Maybe that was his problem. That was the same problem I had that night.

However, as far as a massacre or atrocities were concerned, the 11th Brigade press officer said he neither saw pictures nor heard discussions to that effect. Indeed, when he was asked about the first time he "heard of the My Lai 4 incident as it is now known," Dunn said: "Well, the first time I heard of it was in a story in the paper by Seymour Hersh. That is the first indication I had of it." *Hersh's stories appeared one and a half years later.*

Next in the hierarchy over Haeberle and Roberts was Lt. John W. Moody, information officer for the 11th Brigade. He, too, recalled the disparity between the 128 enemy killed and the small number of weapons captured; but given the nature of the war in Vietnam, he said he did not attach particular significance to it. Moody also acknowledged that he talked to Roberts and Haeberle on the evening of the 16th. What did they tell him?

A. They told me that there was a hell of a big fight and a lot of action, and Haeberle said he had some pictures. They were at that time negatively impressed with what they had seen.

Q. *What do you mean by that?*
A. Well, they didn't like it very well. They were somewhat elated, I think, by having been in contact. It's an exciting thing when there's all that shooting going on, and they seemed to have been affected by that excitement and by the fact that they had gone to the field and been out with troops and this sort of thing. But at the same time, they did not like seeing all the bodies and the killing.

Q. *What kind of bodies?*
A. Of course, I've gone over in mind many times since this

has begun, and can't honestly say that I recall him saying
to me or in my presence that they saw a massacre or that
they saw women and children lined up and shot . . . but
I feel that at the time, what they expressed to me was not
that they had seen a fantastic massacre of women and
children. It was that they had seen a lot of killing and were
somewhat depressed by it. But I heard no accusation from
them in terms of, "We saw the troops killing innocent
people," or any words to that effect.

Q. *Did they tell you that they had seen more than a few bodies
of women and children?*
A. They certainly had told me that they saw a lot of bodies.
I don't believe that they said specifically, "We saw many
bodies of women and children."

Q. *We've talked to both Roberts and to Haeberle.*
A. Yes, sir.

Q. *And Roberts indicated that he was so upset that he couldn't
possibly have written an article about it. Haeberle indicated
he was just sick all over. It seems to me that if they had been
debriefed, this would have come out that they had been
more than a little bit appalled.*
A. Yes, sir. I would have felt so, but perhaps as I say, they
were being hindered by a desire to not sound squeamish.
I don't know. . . .

Moody went on to speculate why he did not receive whatever
"messages," if any, Haeberle and Roberts were trying to send
him that day.

He also was asked whether Haeberle talked to him about the
film he had taken. Replied Moody: "He said he had pictures,
yes, sir. I remember him saying, 'Well, I'll show you pictures,'
but I don't remember him saying they were pictures that would
turn my stomach."

Indeed, Moody said he told Haeberle to develop the pictures
so that they could take a look at the contact prints. But he said

he did not look at all of them, only some. Why not all? Because
he trusted those working for him. When it was pointed out that
it probably would have taken no more than ten minutes a day
for him to look at every picture shot by his photographers, he
said that "I never thought of myself as a detective, and I wasn't
aware of the likelihood of atrocities."

Yet a few of Haeberle's black and white pictures that the
Peers panel had did hint at atrocities, particularly one—Exhibit
P-16—"which shows a burning house with also a couple of
bodies and material on top of one body which is in flames."
When that was shown to Moody in the Pentagon, he agreed he
would have "definitely checked" on it. It was among those
developed at the 11th Brigade when Haeberle returned from My
Lai 4.

Next in the public information hierarchy of the Americal
Division, directly above Moody, was the division information
officer, Lt. Col. Patrick H. Dionne. He did not remember much
about the Son My operation. He did not attend the divisional
briefing at the tactical operations center on March 16 where the
Americal's daily activities were discussed. And, from his attendance at the briefing on the next day, he did not recollect "anything in particular" concerning the maneuvers or the body
count.

Only when a member of the Peers panel pointed out to the
colonel that his own divisional newspaper, the *Americal News
Sheet,* had on March 17 prominently featured the battle in
which 128 of the enemy were reported killed, the colonel said:
"I do remember that 128 figure. I remember the 128 figure, I
really do, because this was the big count. . . ."

That story also stated that only three weapons were captured.
Could the colonel recall any discussions on this disparity? "No,
sir, I do not."

As far as the pictures were concerned, Dionne said he would
see only those that the 11th Brigade decided to forward to his
office.

The Peers panel also pointed out to Dionne that the basis of
what it had heard from other witnesses, there was "much loose

talk" among officers and enlisted men that something unusual
had happened at Son My. Did he ever hear any of it? "No, sir,
I did not." Indeed, Dionne said, "I left Vietnam and I still
wasn't aware that this thing had happened. It was unknown to
me." Not until a year and a half later did the senior information
officer of the American Division, back in the United States, hear
what had happened at Son My.

No Questions Asked

As Haeberle told the Peers inquiry, "At the office, we said a
few things about the women and children and that. I'm positive
I mentioned that, but no one really—the information officer
didn't question me on it, the sergeant didn't question me on it.
No one. They considered it a great success."*

One reason for the sergeant's and the lieutenant's lack of
inquisitiveness was the newness of the operation they were su-
pervising. After all, the 11th Infantry Brigade, whose information office they ran, had arrived in Vietnam only four months
before the My Lai incident to join up with the American Division—which had itself been organized only a few months before,
in mid-1967. Perhaps at the time of My Lai supervision of
information personnel working in the field was still inadequate.

The Peers panel rejected such organizational difficulties as a
blanket excuse for the incident. In its summary report, it points
out that inadequacies in supervision may have contributed to

---

*Haeberle's tour with the army was over a few days after the My Lai
incident. After he was discharged, but before the massacre became
public knowledge, he showed color slides of the incident before "different civic clubs, the Jaycees, Kiwanis Clubs, one high school in the
southern part of Ohio, a church group, youth group," totaling 600 to
1,000 persons in the Cleveland, Ohio, area. According to the testimony,
none of these "substantial citizens," as a panel member described them,
reacted differently from Haeberle's colleague's in the 11th Brigade
information office.

what happened at My Lai but cautions that to "attach undue importance to this fact would involve ignoring similar organizational difficulties faced and successfully resolved by other U.S. army divisions in Vietnam. . . ."[16]

If organizational difficulties were not to blame, perhaps Haeberle's and Robert's superiors were simply too busy fighting a war to pursue the matter properly.

The findings of the Peers panel render this explanation hollow, too. None of Haeberle's and Robert's superiors mention lack of time as a significant problem. To the contrary, one of them, the senior noncommissioned officer of the 11th Brigade information office, agreed that the brigade information officer, Moody, did not spend very much time at his duties when My Lai occurred. As Roberts put it, the brigade information officer "associated loosely" with his office. "He spent very little time in it. He felt, I gather, that we were doing a good job," and the only time he would give instructions was in connection with an assignment. Haeberle described the information officer differently: "He wasn't really that hot of an information officer."

That is not how the Americal Division's deputy information officer, who assumed that position at about the time My Lai occurred, saw the situation. He said he managed to get to the 11th Brigade information office—located about 60 miles from the division's headquarters—about once a month and found its information officer "capable." "It looked like he was running a good shop."

The division's senior information officer, Dionne, did not agree entirely with his deputy. He said he knew the 11th Brigade information officer quite well. For one thing, Dionne said, he visited each of the three brigade information offices "at least once a week." But when one of the panel members asked Dionne whether he agreed that Moody was "somewhat aloof, detached, from the [public information] business," the colonel replied that he got that impression, "but late in the game." Since he had said that he visited the various brigade information offices so frequently, did Dionne know any of the other personnel in the 11th Brigade information office? He said he knew the press officer but

was not close to him. What about the senior sergeant? He
couldn't recall his name, but "I knew him and talked to him,
a little short fellow." Did he know Haeberle and Roberts? No.
He thought he remembered meeting Haeberle several times,
"but it was a situation where I walked in . . . where a lieutenant
was in charge. The enlisted men sort of stayed out of the way
while we had a little conference."

Haeberle agreed that he didn't know the divisional information officer, but disagreed with Dionne on how frequently the
latter visted the 11th Brigade information office. He thought
Dionne had been "in the office a couple of times, but that's all."

Sergeant Stonich said he knew that Dionne was the division
information officer, then a major, but also disagreed that Dionne
visited the 11th Brigade frequently. Had he ever seen Dionne in
his office? "Yes, sir, he came down, I believe once, for a ceremony . . . I believe he was down at Duc Pho [where the 11th
Brigade had its headquarters] one time that I can recall."

Q. *And that was for a ceremony?*
A. Yes, sir.

Q. *Would that have been the change of command ceremony
when [a new commander] took over the brigade?*
A. Yes, sir.

Q. *Did he inspect your shop at that time?*
A. He conducted a visit, sir. It wasn't exactly an inspection.
He walked through. He didn't inspect records or anything
of this nature. He just visited the people in the shop.

Did Roberts know the divisional information officer? "It
might have been Major Hill. I'm not sure. I think he might have
come in later. I'm not sure. No, I think at the time it was a guy,
a major, whose name stated with a 'G.' His first name was Pat.
I don't remember." (His name, of course, was Patrick H.
Dionne, then still a major.)

But perhaps the relationship between the information specialists of the 11th Brigade who were at the scene at My Lai and

the senior information officer for the American Division is not that important because, as Dionne noted, he did not command the various information offices within the division. "They worked for the brigade commander, but all of their information came through my office at division headquarters, everything they provided," he said. Control over them rested with the brigade commander, not the division information officer.

A Lack of Training?

Besides, as Dionne told the Peers panel at another point, "These people were trained in the States before they joined the public information detachment."

But in fact only some the information specialists who appeared before the Peers inquiry had attended the Defense Information School especially set up by the Pentagon to provide at least a modicum of training for its information personnel, or were undergraduate majors in related fields. And even fewer had graduate degrees in such fields, or any kind of related training.

Dionne held a bachelor's degree in history and attended the predecessor of the Defense Information School for eight weeks in 1954 and for nineteen weeks in 1962. He also attended the army's advanced public relations course at the University of Wisconsin.

His deputy, Hill, who later became the American's chief information officer, held a bachelor's degree in physical education and attended the Defense Information School during the year prior to My Lai.

The brigade information officer, Moody, had a bachelor's degree in speech and drama and did not attend the information school. The press officer who worked for Moody—Lieutenant Dunn—had a bachelor's degree in English as well as in journalism and attended the school in 1967. The senior noncommissioned officer of the 11th Brigade, Sergeant Stonich, did not hold an undergraduate degree but had attended the old Army Information School in 1955. Haeberle had majored in fine arts as an undergraduate. He did not go to the Defense Information School. Roberts held a bachelor's degree in business and had not been to the information school. Ford had done some undergraduate work. He did not attend Defense Information School until after May Lai.[17]

The Peers panel, however, was not as interested in the men's training as in the instructions they had received regarding their responsibility to report war crimes. Various inquiry members kept pointing out that the army regulation in force in Vietnam singled out specific personnel, among them photographers, as being responsible for making "every effort to detect the commission of war crimes" and to "report the essential facts to their commanding officer."[18]

The panel asked about that and related regulations as it interrogated the information personnel. Dionne was asked about the Americal Division's rules concerning the burning of houses and huts. He replied that there was a specific order forbidding it. How well was it understood? "I don't know, it was understood at headquarters," he replied. Did he ever instruct his personnel that they should report any violations of rules and regulations and criminal matters to him? No, he met with each man as he reported in but did not discuss this responsibility with them.

Moody was subjected to some vigorous questioning regarding the policy of burning houses and huts. One of his questioners told him: "The policy of the division commander, which has been well cited by many, many people, is that there will be no house burned down without the specific approval of the division commander or, in his absence, an assistant division commander. . . ."

Replied Moody: "That sounds very good, sir. All I can say is that I never heard of that before."

Dunn was asked whether he was ever informed of his obligation to report war crimes and atrocities. He did not recall being told so. What about Haeberle and Roberts? Did Dunn think they would know what the regulation required of them? Dunn was not sure. What about the sergeant who worked for Dunn, Stonich? When asked whether he ever received any instructions concerning his responsibilities to report atrocities and war crimes, he answered, "No, sir, I did not." Did he ever give such instructions to members of his office? "No, sir, I did not." Were the photographers told to report such information? "Not by me, no sir."

Haeberle was read the regulation that specifies the special responsibilities photographers have along with others to report war crimes. He said, "I never had a copy of that, or never even heard of it. Nothing like that was ever mentioned to me." Roberts had the same answer.

Thus it comes perhaps as no surprise that General Peers became rather curt at one point while questioning Dionne. He had just been shown some of the black and white pictures taken and turned in by Haeberle that portrayed the burning of huts and, in one case, two bodies (Exhibit P-16). Dionne said he never saw the pictures, but "I would think that Moody would have called them to my attention." Snapped Peers: "That's exactly why I asked the question, 'Who's running that outfit down there?' "

The "Good News" Syndrome

These information specialists may not have been too familiar with their responsibilities to report war crimes, nor too well trained in the handling of public information, but they did understand one thing: it was not their job to provide negative information about the army.

Roberts: He was asked by the Peers panel whether anyone, including his sergeant, gave him any specific instructions or indoctrination when he joined the information office of the 11th Brigade.

> A. Sergeant Stonich briefed me pretty well. He told me all the Army Regulations that referred to PIO [Public Information Office] and showed me the type of work he was doing and told me basically that we were trying to spread the

name of the 11th Brigade and, you know, make it look as best we could.

Q. *Did he say anything to you about the kind of information that, if it came to your attention, they would want it reported to them?*

A. Well, oftentimes there was information even back in Hawaii that we had to know about, but we certainly didn't report it to anybody. We just knew about it in case we were asked. There were several things that took place, even in Hawaii, such as a man drowning in a training operation. We didn't report that to anybody other than the fact that we knew about it. We had to be knowledgeable in that, if a question was directed to us, you knew what to tell them and what not to tell them.

At another point in the questioning, Roberts provided an example indicating how the good-news-only system worked in connection with one aspect of the My Lai incident. He was asked whether there was any attempt within the information office "to smother any knowledge of this from leaking out?" His answer:

Well, no one in the PIO shop, that I know of, wanted to take it to anybody . . . I know that Sergeant Stonich was concerned that there were pictures in the black and white photos there of hootches being destroyed by fire, and I don't recall specifically which one it was. It may have been the one where the guy is putting a torch to the hootch.

The discussion then veered to the photographs, again including the one showing a burning hut and two bodies. Explained Roberts: ". . . these pictures are the ones that Sergeant Stonich expressed some concern for being taken. He more or less reprimanded Haeberle for taking pictures which were detrimental to the United States Army. . . ."

Or as Roberts put it at another point: "I know we didn't take pictures with an Army camera on black and white of things that we couldn't use, because it was a waste of film and a waste of process time and . . . Sergeant Stonich instructed us not to shoot anything we couldn't use."

Haeberle: At one point he was asked if he ever felt compelled to report what he had seen, either to the inspector general, a legal officer, or to a chaplain. For one thing, he said, no one would believe him. But, interjected General Peers, he had the pictures, particularly the color photos, as proof. If he wanted to use them, why not for "this instead of your own purposes," the general wanted to know. Replied Haeberle:

> You know something, General? If a general is smiling the wrong way in a photograph, I have learned to destroy it. What would happen if I had turned my color in? What would have happened to that? That was my personal work. That would have never gone up there to be developed. My experience as a G.I. over there is that, if something doesn't look right, a general smiling the wrong way . . . I stopped and destroyed the negative. . . .

Stonich: As already noted, Stonich was very frank about his attitude concerning pictures that he felt were not "in keeping with the standards." They were not enlarged nor distributed. He repeated that position again and again in the interrogation.

> Q. *Did you consider that your exclusive function was to develop favorable news for the 11th Brigade, in a favorable light with the public and with other areas?*
> A. Yes, sir. I like to put them favorably if the instances arose. If the situation arose unfavorable, I wouldn't hesitate to give it the same coverage as it would be if favorable. Of course, truthfully, I wouldn't feel that it would be released, but I would give it the same coverage.

Dunn: The brigade press officer painted a very clear picture of the role of public information in the Americal Division. His testimony is particularly pertinent, not only because he had a

bachelor's degree in journalism and went through the Defense
Information School before going to Vietnam, but because he had
also worked as a newspaper reporter. He was asked if he could
describe for the Peers inquiry what the functions of his office
were. He listed two: to distribute information from above to the
troops and to provide information about the brigade—in the
form of stories and pictures—to higher headquarters.

Q. *. . . would it be fair to say that your function was to provide
higher headquarters with good information about most of
the brigade?*
A. Certainly. Yes, sir.

Q. *In other words, you didn't perform the function of finding
information of all kinds and transmitting it to higher headquarters that you performed for* The Chicago Tribune?
A. That is exactly right. There is a fine line there between those
two: my job in the brigade, and my job at *The Tribune.*

Q. *You said there is a difference?*
A. There certainly is.

Q. *Now, I would like for you to be a little more specific about
it. For example, during the course of your service in the
office, the brigade information office, did you ever have
occasion to report information which might be called derogatory or unfavorable information about the brigade?*
A. Did you say, did I ever have occasion to do it?

Q. *Yes. Did you do it?*
A. I never did it.

Q. *Would it be fair to say that if, to assume that if Mr. Roberts
had presented you with an article on this operation that
began something like, "Task Force Barker today got something like 128 VC and a few children along with it," you
would immediately "blue pencil" the part about the few
children? Is that a fair estimate of how you would have
reacted in view of your concept of your function?*

A. Yes, sir. There would have been no reason to move this information along.

Q. *Because it did not reflect favorably upon—?*

A. [Interposing] Also, it would have been "blue penciled" at a higher level, and they would have called us and said: "What the hell are you doing sending this kind of information up through channels?"

Q. *Did such an occasion ever occur where you included something that reflected unfavorably upon division?*

A. It happened. I can't say when. There were occasions of differences of opinion that we had with division. I don't know whether these differences referred to derogatory stories—never derogatory stories. People in our offices had been trained at the information school. They knew what was asked of them, what was required of them. I had been trained there and I knew.

Q. *In the course of that training, are you given instruction that the function that you perform is not to transmit unfavorable information about your unit, but only favorable information?*

A. I can't say that that type of training is in the doctrine of the information school, but it is certainly understood.

Q. *Was that concept made clear to Sergeant Haeberle and Specialist Roberts when they were in your organization?*

A. I don't know whether we ever sat down and said: "Now listen, fellows, if you see something that is nasty, don't write it or don't photograph it." As I say, the concept was understood. There was no mistake about it. They knew it, I knew it, and Lieutenant Moody knew it.

Q. *Would it be a fair characterization of your understanding of your office's function to say that it acted as a public relations office normally does in private life?*

A. Sir, I have no personal knowledge of public relations functions. But to my understanding, that is exactly what we were. We also operated as liaison in case there were any civilian news people in the area. We were escorts as such. But I think the public relations function would be—that was pretty much our job.

Moody: The brigade information officer was less outspoken before the Peers panel, although he also made it clear that untoward pictures would not be released. However, when Moody testified at the trial of the former commander of the 11th Brigade, he echoed Dunn's views.

> Q. *And the IO shop there, your IO shop, had received pretty explicit instructions that you were not there to report and publicize adverse allegations against the Brigade? What you were to send out was in the form of public relations for the Brigade?*
> A. As a matter of fact, that was just about the first in-country lesson I received. As soon as we arrived in Vietnam, the Division information officer called for me and the first things that he found to tell me were in that regard.

Indeed, a few moments later, Moody agreed before the court-martial that if bad news were sent to higher levels, it would never be published.[19]

Dionne: The former chief information officer of the American Division agreed with Moody. Dionne was asked by the Peers panel whether "it is fair to say that the primary, if not exclusive, function of the information section to the various units was to find and report favorable information that would meet the [U.S. Military Assistance Command, Vietnam] requirements for release to the public?" "Yes, sir. I think so," replied Dionne.

Subsequent Handling of Information about the My Lai Incident

In view of the American Division's information specialists approach to the handling of public information, it is hardly surprising that Haeberle's and Roberts's superiors claim not to have been aware that a massacre had taken place right under their noses. But their protestations of ignorance strain credulity, particularly since a soldier not even assigned to the Americal Division managed to hear about My Lai within six weeks. What he heard from a G.I. whom he had known in the United States and who was assigned to C Company, 11th Brigade, Americal Division, so upset him that he decided to find out more. By June, he had located four more members of C Company who had been at My Lai. And each one confirmed what the others had said.[20]

When the G.I., Ronald Ridenhour, was discharged from the army in December 1968 and returned to Phoenix, Arizona, he pondered what to do with the information he had. He decided to write a letter to 30 members of Congress, the White House, and other executive branch officials.

That triggered an army investigation which led to charges being placed against Lieutenant Calley. At this point the Defense Department decided to make the innocuous release from remote Fort Benning rather than from the Pentagon—which normally releases all information of national or international consequence—that Calley was being charged with the murder of Vietnamese civilians. That release failed to mention that Calley was being charged with deliberately shooting dozens of Vietnamese civilians.

The Pentagon was prepared for a flood of inquiries from the press. Former Defense Secretary Melvin Laird "later revealed that he had ordered the news wires monitored to see if the announcement would spark immediate controversy."[21]

It did not. Among the few reporters who made an attempt to follow up on the story was a military writer for the Columbus, Georgia, *Enquirer,* but Calley refused to discuss the case with him at nearby Fort Benning. Calley's hometown newspaper, the Miami *Herald,* had one of its experienced reporters follow up on the meager wire service story that had carried the announcement of the charges against Calley. The reporter called the Fort Benning information officer to find out how many persons Calley was accused of having murdered. "No comment," was the answer. The reporter wrote a story on the matter, published inside the *Herald,* and dropped the matter.

Meanwhile, Ridenhour felt that the army was dragging its feet. Fearing that no one other than Calley would be so much as reprimanded, he contacted a Washington reporter for the Phoenix, Arizona, *Republic.* The reporter was not interested. But the military writer for the Columbus *Enquirer* had remained curious after being brushed off by Calley. He had noticed Calley's American Division patch. By talking to other veterans of that division stationed at Fort Benning, the writer had pieced together many of the important details of the case. He did not publish his story, however, because "he didn't want to embarrass the Army."[22] Eventually, the New York *Times* and the Washington *Post* received tips about the case, but nothing came of them.

On October 22, 1969, Seymour Hersh, former Pentagon correspondent for the AP, then a freelance writer finishing a book on the military, also received a tip. He followed it up, first, by flying to Salt Lake City to see Calley's attorney, second, by flying to Fort Benning to find Calley—and to get him to talk. He did.[23]

Hersh wrote his first story and tried to get *Life* and *Look* to publish it. Neither was interested. It was subsequently distributed to 30 newspapers in mid-November 1968 through the bantam Dispatch News Service. Still, the American press was slow to follow up on the story. The New York *Times* and some others pursued the story to Vietnam, but little was done domestically. Hersh kept working on it, and his articles continued to appear—as did some of Haeberle's photographs of the massacre. The Cleveland *Plain Dealer* published several late in November 1969. More appeared in color in *Life* magazine later. With that, plus television interviews of former members of C Company, the story made the covers of *Time* and *Newsweek.*[24]

At this point General Peers was appointed to determine how thorough the original investigations of the My Lai 4 incident had been. Not only did the Peers inquiry find that elements of the American Division had "massacred a large number of Vietnamese nationals in the village of Son My"; it also found that the original investigations had been "superficial and misleading" and that efforts to conceal or withhold information were widespread.[25]

And the panel found out that My Lai 4 had not been the only scene of a massacre on March 16, 1968. A smaller incident had occurred at another hamlet within Son My village, My Khe 4.

But when Peers was asked at that Pentagon press conference about other atrocities, the general choose to say nothing about the My Khe 4 killings. Indeed, according to Seymour Hersh, after the conference Peers stopped by the office of a colleague and, referring to the three hours of prepping by Pentagon public relations personnel, complained: "Three hours of hell and there wasn't a tough question asked."[26]

In ironic contrast, among the individuals the Peers inquiry cited for "ommissions and commissions" in connection with what happened at Son My were Ronald Haeberle and Jay Roberts. Both were accused of failing to try to stop the atrocities and to report what they had seen to their superiors. Haeberle was also accused of withholding photographic evidence and Roberts of preparing "an article for the brigade newspaper which omitted all mention of the war crimes he had observed" and of giving "a false and misleading account of the Task Force Barker Operation."[27]

Yet nowhere in its report does the Peers panel point to the dismal consequences of the favorable-news-only policy so widely adhered to by the Americal Division's information personnel. Indeed, its questions of the information specialists indicate no serious qualms about that policy at all.

Other questions seemingly important to an inquiry into the suppression or withholding of information about the My Lai incident were not even asked. For instance, what effect did the military's preoccupation with secrecy have on the way the bad —but unclassified—news about the massacre was handled? What sort of obligation did the involved public officials, from sergeants to secretaries of defense, feel they had in the handling of the information? What role did that all-important military figure, the commanding officer, play in the process?

The testimony of the Americal's public relations specialists clearly hinted that these and other factors might have been at work in the handling of the news about the My Lai incident, but none of the clues was seriously pursued.

The Peers report did not even question why these PR specialists did not practice what the Defense Information School so piously preaches about the handling of news, be it good or bad: maximum disclosure with minimum delay.

But then, neither did the Inquiry's chief when he met the press.

2

Three
Intertwining
Trends

If the Peers inquiry testimony illustrates the hiding of the Pentagon, a Columbia Broadcasting System documentary in 1971 dramatically portrayed the other side of the same coin.

Ten months in the making, it opened with scenes showing U.S. Marines on maneuvers, in view of an audience of invited civilians. Narrator Roger Mudd observed that the mock battle was more than a military exercise: ". . . it was also an exercise in salesmanship—the selling of the Pentagon."

The program's 9.5 million viewers were told that the Defense Department budget lists $30 million for these explanatory and promotional public relations efforts, but that outsiders estimate the "real total at $190 million."

Whatever the exact amount might be, CBS showed how the money is spent:

On Armed Forces Day demonstrations of military equipment. ("The Army Exhibit Unit has been to 239 cities in 46 states and has been seen by over 20 million people. The cost to the taxpayers: $906,000 a year.")

On "teams of colonels" who tour the country lecturing

civilians and military reservists on defense and foreign policy. The teams, according to the documentary, have addressed 180,000 persons in 163 cities during three years.

On special guided tours of military installations and equipment for 3,000 carefully selected civilians who get to fire rifles and to drive tanks.

On more than 300 films the military produces each year at a cost of more than $12 million, many of which are not merely used for troop information but are shown to the general public and ". . . contain a high proportion of propaganda. . . ."

On news films Pentagon crews shot in Vietnam for distribution to American television stations, some of which, former military men claim, are staged.

On information officers who see to it, for example, that a network crew doing a documentary on the air war in Indochina talks only to carefully selected pilots.[1]

Reaction to the broadcast was strong. Those who praised it included the National Academy of Television Arts and Sciences, which honored "The Selling of the Pentagon" with an "Emmy," and the Peabody Prize committee, which selected it for its prestigious award.

Those who criticized the program included F. Edward Hébert, then still chairman of the House Armed Services Committee, then Vice President Spiro T. Agnew and, to a lesser degree, Melvin Laird, at the time the secretary of defense.

Indeed, the reaction was so strong that CBS decided to rebroadcast the documentary, appending to it 20 minutes of comments by Hébert, Agnew, and Laird, plus a counterpoint by the president of CBS News.

The main target of the critics was not the veracity of CBS's allegations about the extent and nature of Pentagon PR. Instead, they attacked the network's editing practices, which they claimed distorted the program. Although the Federal Communications Commission could find no evidence to support those charges, the House Commerce Committee pursued the issue in extended hearings. When CBS refused to produce some material gathered for the broadcast but not shown on the air, the committee threatened to hold the president of CBS in contempt. The issue abated only after the full House refused to support its Commerce Committee.[2]

The momentary tempest churned up by the CBS documentary was surprising if only because most of what the network reported was not news. As long ago as the early 1950s the Defense Department's public relations activities were lambasted for being too self-serving.[3] Academics and others from left[4] to right[5] on the political spectrum commented on Pentagon PR efforts in the ensuing years. Even Mr. Hébert had been known to complain long before the airing of the CBS program about the "pusillanimous propaganda" that he claimed was being generated by the "well known . . . propaganda machine of the Pentagon."[6]

But the scope of the Pentagon's explanatory and promotional public relations activities were exposed in greatest detail in a series of speeches delivered in the U.S. Senate in 1969.[7] In those speeches and in a subsequent book, Senator J. William Fulbright said that there are approximately 2,800 civilians and military personnel "whose job is selling the public on the Department of Defense, the individual military services, and their appropriations," at a cost, as of 1969, of $27,953,000 annually. The senator said that these Pentagon-supplied figures were, "to put it mildly, conservative," an assessment the General Accounting Office would later second.[8] (Indeed, in a subsequent report to the Senate Appropriations Committee, the Pentagon itself listed the number of personnel engaged in public relations work at 4,430, at an annual cost of $44,062,000.[9]) Fulbright, then still chairman of the Senate Foreign Relations Committee, went on to describe the activities on which these funds are spent, including some the CBS documentary subsequently only touched on and a variety of others it left out entirely.

The Rise of Public Relations
in the U.S. Armed Forces

Given that kaleidoscopic range of Pentagon public relations activities, the findings of a survey of federal publicity practices conducted on the eve of World War II are startling. It found the military departments to be among those agencies having the *least* elaborate array of public information activities.[10]

It is, of course, not exactly new to find that military men relay information about their actions to their superiors and, through them, to the public. That practice appears to be as old as war itself. However, until the time of Napoleon Bonaparte, these reports were usually straightforward, often tediously detailed "bulletins" of the actions in which a particular army or navy had been engaged. Napoleon changed that practice drastically, turning battle dispatches into propagandistic bulletins aimed at firing up troops on the field, shoring up support on the home front, and demoralizing the enemy.[11]

In the early days of the United States, the armed forces generally followed the pre-Napoleonic practice of limiting their information activities to the transmission of reports from generals in the field to the superiors back in the capital. The dissemination of public information similar to the Pentagon's current practices did not occur until the turn of this century, when the War Department, at the request of a reporter, started to post daily information for the press about the conduct of the Spanish-American War on a bulletin board in Washington.

With PR on the rise in the private sector, it took only the pressures of World War I for public relations to be formally recognized by the military. During World War I the two predecessors of today's Department of Defense—the War and Navy Departments—set up public information offices as part of their intelligence branches.[12] A second event important to the evolution of military information practices also took place during the First World War: the creation by President Woodrow Wilson of the Committee on Public Information. Headed by George Creel, its main job was to build broad public support for the war effort—to "sell the war."[13]

Once that war was won, PR continued its rapid growth outside of the military. But within the armed forces, whose ranks shrunk sharply as the country demobilized, public relations nearly withered away. Only when the lights began to go out in Europe did the American military slowly start crawling out of its shell once more. By 1941 that led to the elevation of PR from its subordinate position within military intelligence to the level of the secretary of the army as well as the navy.[14]

In this war too, the president set up an information organization outside the armed forces to mobilize support for the war effort. It was the job of the Office of War Information, its director, Elmer Davis, said, "not only to tell the American people how the war is going, but where it is going and where it came from."[15]

But this time military PR did not wither away. In the months following the war's end all the services retained their information offices at the top of their organizational hierarchies, directly under the secretary. When the air force became an independent service in 1947, it did the same. Indeed, following unification of the services with the National Security Act of 1947, the importance ascribed to public relations was reflected in the establishment of a public affairs section at the apex of the Department of Defense hierarchy, in the office of the secretary of defense.

The defense secretary's Office of Public Information became increasingly powerful as a result of the mounting competition among the individual services for defense dollars and the concomitant use of PR as a tactic to win support for their divergent positions. The first two Defense secretaries reacted to the interservice publicity battles by moving many of the public information specialists from the services into their own office. The Korean War interrupted this centralization, and PR continued to be a weapon in the internecine strife that plagued the Defense Department during much of the 1950s.[16]

In line with the Kennedy administration's overall attempt to centralize federal information activities,[17] Secretary of Defense Robert S. McNamara quickly bridled the department's public information activities by pulling them together in his office. Today the office of the assistant secretary of defense for public affairs oversees all defense public information efforts. In the 1950s Congress limited the Defense Department and the services to spending $2,755,000 on public relations and information activities, but no such ceiling has existed since 1960.[18] Today the Pentagon pegs its public affairs costs at $24 million: even using this official figure, expenditures for Defense Department public relations have increased roughly ninefold in 15 years.

The Evolution of Restrictive
Information Practices

If it is surprising that the military's public information activities were not long ago among the least elaborate in Washington, then the findings of another prewar study are astounding. In a survey of Washington correspondents, this study found none who complained that the intentional withholding or distorting of information was a major problem in covering the capital.[19]

The military's policy of enshrouding its operations in secrecy to prevent the enemy from gaining undue advantage is, of course, ancient. Such curtailing of information has probably always gone beyond keeping only purely military affairs secret; yet major problems did not arise until European journalists started to accompany armies into the field during the first half of the nineteenth century. What the correspondents reported did not always agree with the commanding general's assessment. Consequently, "it became almost the habit of officers to handle disagreeable journalists with the riding whip." On the other hand, military men of the time did not mind bribing agreeable journalists—with money or with scoops—if they thought it would help to boost public morale.[20]

The American government's efforts to keep military operations secret began with the Revolutionary War.[21] By the time of the Civil War, American journalists, like their European counterparts, accompanied the army into the field. Moreover, the telegraph now made it possible for information to be disseminated far and fast. As a result, censorship of war news arrived in the United States when the government in Washington took control of the telegraph wires[22]—sparking charges that more than military information was being blue-penciled. A congressional investigation eventually found that "dispatches, almost numberless, of political, personal, and general character, have been suppressed by the censor."[23]

As wars grew, so did efforts to keep the lid on information. During World War I the withholding of information deemed militarily important was the job of the armed forces and George Creel's Committee on Public Information. The army, in addition to classifying information under its own control at home, invoked censorship on the battlefields abroad. The Creel Committee, meanwhile, screened information both within the United States and emanating from the United States, designated for dissemination abroad. Although Creel relied primarily on voluntary compliance, his committee's efforts were buttressed by the various sedition and espionage acts the postmaster general and the attorney general invoked to restrict civil liberties—acts aimed primarily at the socialist and German-language press.[24] With the war's end, censorship of military information ended as America's armed forces returned to their traditional peacetime status: small and publicity-shy.

However, within 10 days of the Japanese attack on Pearl Harbor, the nation had a new director of censorship, Byron Price. A new law empowered Price to censor all communications going abroad. To control information inside the country, President Franklin D. Roosevelt asked Price to coordinate the American media's completely voluntary effort to withhold information that could be valuable to the enemy.[25]

Price, like Creel, was an experienced newsman. But whereas Creel was both chief censor and chief propagandist, and thus afflicted with the temptation to withhold or distort information because it was in conflict with the parallel propaganda effort, Price was concerned only with security. The intentional manipulation of public opinion was outside his domain.[26]

Shortly after its inception, the Office of Censorship published its "Code of Wartime Practices for the American Press." Revised several times, it was always a small document, never more than a dozen five-by-eight-inch pages long.[27] It spelled out the information that could not be disseminated without "appropriate authority": location of troops, planes, and ships, production contracts and capacities, casualty reports, ship sinkings. But even these matters could be published if the "appropriate authority"—for example, the navy in the case of a ship sunk by the enemy—gave its approval.[28] Security was narrowly defined as only those matters that clearly hurt the military prosecution of the war.

At the end of that war, Price spelled out the principles on which the code was based:

> Voluntary censorship must deal only with questions involving security.
>
> It must never base a request on any security consideration which may be questionable. The danger to security must be real, and must be backed by a solid and reasonable explanation.
>
> It must avoid any interference whatever with editorial opinion. . . .
>
> It must never be influenced by non-security considerations of policy or public needs. . . .
>
> It must make no requests which would put the press in the position of policing or withholding from publication the utterances of responsible public officials.
>
> It must make every effort to avoid multiple censorship and on no account must withhold from the American public any information which has been generally disseminated abroad.
>
> It must operate openly, advising of every request made of the press.[29]

The code was cussed and criticized, but, aided by strong public support of the war, it generally worked well. Under it, no significant attempts by government to hide blunders came to light and no security breaches of consequence were committed by the press.[30] And with the surrender of Japan the Office of Censorship promptly went out of business.

But the notion of censoring an ever-growing amount of defense information survived. Various proposals cropped up that would have extended the withholding of information far beyond Price's definition of security. In 1947, for example, the Security Advisory Board of the State Department-Army-Navy-Air Force Coordinating Committee came up with a classification scheme that would have banned the use of information that might cause "serious administrative embarrassment." A year later, Defense Secretary James Forrestal tried unsuccessfully to have the media voluntarily withhold "information detrimental to our national security."[31]

In the midst of the Korean War, President Harry Truman decided the time had come to settle the issue by formalizing a sweeping security classification system. He issued an executive order authorizing all federal agencies to mark information they considered sensitive either "top secret," "secret," "confidential," or "restricted."[32]

The Truman order proved very unpopular, particularly with the press. It was vague; it allowed too many individuals to wield the secrecy stamp; it could be used to cover up personal and political mistakes. In response, President Dwight D. Eisenhower in 1953 limited the number of classifications to three (abolishing "restricted" as a category), curtailed the number of agencies that could classify information, and restricted somewhat the authority that agency heads could delegate. But the order's definitions remained ambiguous, and the declassification process it prescribed was ineffective.

Yet it remained in effect for nearly 20 years. In the aftermath of the publication of the Pentagon Papers, Richard M. Nixon in 1972 issued a new order outlining the classification system currently in effect. Executive Order 11652 further limits the number of agencies authorized to classify information and the individuals who can restrict material. It also seeks to speed up the declassification process.[33]

This formalized postwar classification system has resulted in a huge amount of material that is being withheld for security reasons. In the Defense Department, the volume is such that no one knows how much classified material there is. A top Pentagon administrator did give a House committee a rough estimate, saying that department's biennial records reports show that it has approximately 6 million cubic feet of active files. Of that, "approximately 17 per cent represent classified documents of all classification levels."[34] In other words, 1,020,000 cubic feet of the Pentagon's files current at the time were classified.*

The present classification system has few defenders. One critic, former Supreme Court Justice Arthur Goldberg, told a congressional committee that he had read and himself prepared thousands of restricted papers. "In my experience, 75 per cent of these documents should never have been classified in the first place; another 15 per cent quickly outlived the need for secrecy; and only about 10 per cent genuinely required restricted access for any significant period of time."[35]

A former Defense Department security classification specialist, William G. Florence, who spent 43 years working for the federal government as a military officer and as a civilian, was even harsher in his estimate before the same committee: "I sincerely believe that less than one-half of one per cent of the different documents which bear currently assigned classification markings actually contain information qualifying even for the lowest defense classification. . . ."[36]

Even former President Nixon was not happy with the system. It, he said, "has frequently served to conceal bureaucratic mistakes or to prevent embarrassment to officials and administrations" and has allowed "too many papers to be classified for too long a time."[37]

Dozens of examples can be found in the relevant literature and congressional hearings to support this viewpoint. One will

---

*As author David Wise figures it, if converted into linear feet, that amounts to 2,297 stacks, each as high as the 555-foot Washington Monument.

suffice. During a 1972 hearing, the chairman of the House Sub-committee on Foreign Operations and Government Information asked the general counsel of the Defense Department the date of the oldest classified document the department had. Counsel didn't know, but promised to find out. In due course, the committee received his reply: "It appears that the oldest document is likely to be a 1912 contingency plan, currently classified 'Confidential,' on the grounds that its contents could be exploited for purposes prejudicial to current national security interests."[38]

Only time will tell whether the Nixon executive order will change a system that restricts a document prepared five dozen years ago. However, in view of the relatively minor modifications it contains, two students of the classification process are not optimistic. They describe the new order as "more political than potent," likely to disappoint those who had hoped for considerably freer access to government documents.[39]

Less Formal Efforts to Limit National Security Information

It might be assumed that the establishment of this massive, formal security classification system would have meant the end of informal efforts to stem the flow of information from the Pentagon to the public. After all, not only the Defense Department but also other agencies involved in "national security" matters now had broad, presidentially granted authority to restrict information at the source, even in peacetime.

That stopped none of the overzealous censors. Over time, their efforts increased—sharply.

One of the first major moves in that direction occurred in 1954 when the secretary of commerce, with presidential approval, created the Office of Strategic Information. It was to work with business in "voluntary efforts to prevent unclassified information from being made available to those foreign nations which might use the data in a manner harmful to the United

States." The press objected loudly, particularly the trade and technical publications, but the office remained in business until 1957.[40]

A similar attempt was made by former Defense Secretary Charles E. Wilson in 1955. He ordered that all material Defense personnel planned to publish had to be reviewed and cleared. The censors were directed not only to look for security violations but also to determine "whether release or publication of the material would constitute a constructive contribution to the primary mission of the Department of Defense." That directive remained on the books for three years.[41]

As if that did not suffice, Wilson's deputy assistant secretary of defense for public affairs also called on the press in 1955 to "voluntarily refrain from publishing information that is not secret but might be helpful to the Russians."[42]

The media did not take kindly to these attempts to extend the withholding of information beyond classified material. The Associated Press Managing Editors Association, for example, said it "expressly condemns" such practices.[43]

If the press would not voluntarily refrain from disseminating "unconstructive" information involving "national security," the government had other options—to lie, for instance.

When the Soviet Union claimed in 1960 that it had shot down a high-flying American U-2 spy plane, the United States responded by saying that one of its weather research planes was missing. It may have drifted over the USSR, it was suggested. A government spokesman, meanwhile, insisted before the American public that there was "absolutely no—N-O—deliberate attempt to violate Soviet air space. . . ." But then the Soviet Union produced the plane's pilot and said he had confessed to having been on an intelligence mission over the USSR. Only then did the government back down and admit the spy flights.[44]

Other efforts were made to keep unclassified information from being disseminated because it was deemed not to be in the "national interest." Within a year of the U-2 incident, for example, *The New Republic* accepted "without questions" President John F. Kennedy's suggestion not to run an article on CIA activities among Cuban refugees in preparation for the Bay of Pigs invasion.[45] Without a presidential "suggestion" the New York *Times* decided to considerably soften similar stories gathered by its correspondent.[46]

Addressing members of the American Newspaper Publishers Association shortly after the 1961 Bay of Pigs invasion had failed, Kennedy spelled out clearly what he saw as the press's duty to refrain voluntarily from publishing some material:* "Every newspaper now asks itself with respect to every story: 'Is it news?' All I suggest is that you add the question: 'Is it in the interest of national security?' "[47]

Another president's formal statement, also addressed to a major press association but made a mere 20 years earlier, shows clearly just how much attitudes at the highest level of American government have changed on the question of "national security." A few months before Pearl Harbor—a time when Washington was rife with rumors that the administration would seek to invoke compulsory censorship in view of the hot war spreading in Europe—President Roosevelt wrote the American Society of Newspaper Editors:

> Suppression of opinion and censorship of news are among the mortal weapons that dictatorships direct against their own people and against the world. As far as I am concerned there will be no government control of news unless it be of vital military information. . . . It would be a shameful abuse of patriotism to suggest that opinion should be stifled in its service.[48]

And during the war that followed no system of compulsory censorship was instituted within the United States. To the contrary, when the media, in reaction to pressure from unauthor-

---

*Ironically, according to Clifton Daniel of the *Times,* Kennedy privately told executives of that newspaper that he wished they had printed all they knew of the Bay of Pigs invasion prior to its launching because "you would have saved us from a colossal mistake."

ized self-appointed military and civilian censors, began to delete
more information than asked, the country's only official censor,
Byron Price, chewed out the zealots:

> There is abundant evidence that newspapers and radio sta-
> tions are suppressing news for no valid reason. . . . In addition
> to your loyal and generally excellent cooperation under the
> voluntary code, many of you have been led to overzealousness
> to withhold information having no security value.
>
> . . . I am sure that neither the publishing industry nor the
> broadcasting industry wants to abrogate its responsibility to
> disseminate all news which does not violate national security.
>
> I solicit your continued cooperation to see, in this instance,
> that a dangerous psychology of over-censorship is not created
> throughout the land by the activities of a miscellany of volun-
> teer firemen.[49]

Thus spoke the head of the office that helped keep the lid on
such vital military secrets as the atomic bomb and the proximity
fuse in the middle of the hottest war in which this country has
ever been engaged.

Yet 20 years later, in time of cold war, Price and his deputy
of wartime days, Theodore F. Koop, were summoned to the
White House in the Bay of Pigs aftermath to explore with two
of Kennedy's top aides the feasibility of voluntary censorship of
one kind or another. Both argued against such a move, claiming
that in peacetime the country would not accept it.[50]

Kennedy's efforts to control "national security" information
did not stop there; he next called in seven top news executives
to discuss the subject. Pierre Salinger, Kennedy's news secretary, recalls that the meeting was a "total failure." The media
brass bluntly told the president that in the absence of a declared
national emergency, "they would accept no new security restrictions—voluntary or official."[51]

But Kennedy's views on national security information were
shared by his secretary of defense. Robert S. McNamara indicated where he stood on the issue before the Senate Armed

Services Committee in 1961 when he posed this question: "Why should we tell Russia that the Zeus [antimissile system] developments may be unsatisfactory?" His answer: "What we ought to be saying is that we have the most perfect anti-ICBM system that the human mind will ever devise."[52]

McNamara brought in Arthur Sylvester as his assistant for public affairs. He made his position very clear by such actions as ordering all Pentagon personnel to report the content of every interview and telephone call with a reporter to a public information officer.[53] This much-criticized 1962 directive remained in force until Sylvester quit the department five years later.

But Sylvester did some other things before leaving the Pentagon. After the Cuban Missile Crisis, during which reporters felt Sylvester had engaged in some questionable information practices,[54] he issued a statement in which he said news in the hands of government is "part of the arsenal of weaponry that a president has" to deal with a crisis. Later that year, he was more outspoken on the subject before a professional journalism meeting in New York. "It would seem to me, basic, all through history . . . that it's inherent in the government's right, if necessary, to lie to save itself when it's going up into a nuclear war."[55]

The press howled with protest; Sylvester reacted by denying he ever made the remark. But the American Broadcasting Company had taped the speech—and the transcript shows that the "right-to-lie" crack was made.[56] It was not until 1967, after he had left the Pentagon, that Sylvester finally owned up to it under his byline in an article entitled, "The Government Has the Right to Lie."[57]

Just how strongly he felt about that right, however, is better reflected in a comment he made to American correspondents in Saigon in 1966: "Look, if you think any American official is going to tell you the truth, then you're stupid. Did you hear that? Stupid."[58]

Or as Maxwell Taylor, former chairman of the Joint Chiefs of Staff and onetime ambassador to South Vietnam said less bluntly after publication of the Pentagon Papers a few years later: "A citizen should know those things he needs to know to be a good citizen and discharge his functions . . . not to get in on secrets which simply damage his government and indirectly damage the citizen himself."[59]

Despite these sentiments at the top levels of the U.S. government, the World War II–initiated trend of restricting an ever-increasing amount of information—particularly national security information—did not proceed entirely unopposed. In large part, the executive branch itself brought on this opposition through its broad interpretation of the 1946 Administrative Procedures Act. It stated, for example, that records shall "be made available to persons properly and directly concerned," unless the information needed to be "held confidential for good cause found." Unfortunately, the act left it to the bureaucracy to determine when someone was "properly and directly concerned" and what constituted "good cause" to keep a document under wraps. The abuses that resulted were instrumental in the formation in 1955 of a special House subcommittee on government information whose efforts over the next dozen years led to the 1967 Freedom of Information Act.[60] The act tried to specify what records anyone—rather than only "persons properly and directly concerned"—should be able to obtain routinely from the executive branch. It exempted nine categories of information, ranging from national defense secrets to certain geological data. A product of much political compromise, the act was attacked for its vagueness almost from the day it became law.[61]

In 1971, the House Foreign Operations and Government Information Subcommittee, into which the special panel of the 1950s had evolved, held a series of hearings to see how the Freedom of Information Act had fared. Prodded by the Pentagon Papers controversy, the hearings spilled over into 1972 and confirmed the array of criticisms leveled at the act. It became obvious that the loopholes that riddled the legislation had been used by the bureaucracy to thwart the law's intent. It needed to be overhauled.[62]

Late in 1974, Congress did just that by tacking a string of amendments on to the 1967 version. The amendments limit the time within which federal agencies must respond to information requests; judges can now review material *in camera* to determine whether or not it should be released; information seekers who have to go to court to dislodge a record may now be reimbursed for "reasonable attorney fees and other litigation costs" if they are upheld; and in cases where the judge finds that the information was withheld "arbitrarily or capriciously," the U.S. Civil Service Commission can now even discipline the errant public servant.

President Gerald Ford vetoed the amendments when they reached his desk. Congress, however, was not to be denied in the post-Watergate atmosphere. It overrode the veto, and the amendments became law in 1975. The strengthened act has since been invoked much more frequently, and its new teeth are helping to pry larger chunks of information out of the executive branch, including some revelations deeply embarrassing to the CIA and the FBI, agencies that were virtually untouchable only a few years earlier. Despite these promising beginnings, it will take years to determine whether the act genuinely affects the way the Pentagon handles bad news.

Beyond the Norm: The Handling of Bad News

Between Pearl Harbor and Vietnam, then, two trends clearly emerged in the way the American military handled information about itself. On the one hand, the Pentagon enthusiastically followed American business and industry and adopted public relations as a strategy for selling its product and garnering public support; on the other, it vastly expanded its activities aimed at restricting the flow of information.

The effort to limit and control more and more information proceeded along separate but parallel paths. One avenue involved the formal authority the Defense Department was given —even in the absence of a declaration of war—to classify enormous amounts of information on the basis of very elastic standards. The other, the more informal approach, was shaped as

much by directives as by examples set by officials ranking as
high as the commander-in-chief. These made it clear that it was
acceptable—in the name of national security—to manipulate
information that is neither classified nor otherwise legitimately
suppressible.

Amid these efforts by the Pentagon to burnish its image and
to bar data deemed injurious to national security, a third major
trend emerged: the manipulation of bad news. The My Lai
incident exemplifies this third trend all too vividly. It shows
clearly that Defense officials do try to withhold or distort newsworthy information seen as inimical to the department's interests.[63]

Unfortunately, My Lai was not an anomaly. Other cases are
not difficult to pinpoint:

> When General John D. Lavelle ordered unauthorized
> raids on military targets in North Vietnam, the Defense De-
> partment tried to conceal them; and when Lavelle was fired,
> the air force announced he was retiring for reasons of health.[64]
> A commander of the Washington military district
> claimed that for reasons of "military secrecy" he withheld "a
> letter pressuring liquor lobbyists and wholesalers to provide
> free drinks for 1,200 guests at an Army St. Valentine's Day
> party."[65]
> The Office of International Security Affairs resurrected
> in 1970 the practice that press phone calls could not be ac-
> cepted without prior clearance from public information offi-
> cials. It also mandated that face-to-face interviews had to be
> monitored. When reporters asked to see the directive, even
> that was denied—until a suit under the Freedom of Informa-
> tion Act was threatened.[66]
> On the basis of the Pentagon's and the administration's
> claims that North Vietnamese torpedo boats had attacked
> two destroyers, Congress passed the 1964 Gulf of Tonkin
> resolution empowering the president to retaliate. It thereafter
> was used as an *ipso facto* declaration of war. Subsequent
> events showed that to obtain support for the resolution, de-
> fense officials and others in the executive branch withheld and
> distorted critical information.[67]
> A freelance writer was told by West Point that two

manuals pertaining to the school's freshman military training program—often criticized for including hazing—would not be released because they were "documents which provide only internal guidance to Department of Defense personnel."[68] Shortly afterward, both manuals were publicly available in full as part of a House Armed Services Committee hearing.[69]

Perhaps the most prominent case is that involving the Pentagon Papers, the 7,000-page study commissioned in 1967 by Secretary of Defense McNamara. The papers show again and again that administration after administration talked differently in public than in private.[70]

The U.S.S. *Liberty* was attacked by Israeli aircraft and torpedo boats during the 1967 Mideast war, leaving 34 American sailors dead and another 75 wounded. When asked to explain what the ship was doing so close to the fighting, Pentagon officials replied the *Liberty* was there "to assure communications between U.S. Government posts in the Middle East and to assist in relaying information concerning the evacuation of American dependent and other American citizens. . . ." That answer was less than accurate. The *Liberty*, it turned out, was a spy ship monitoring the two sides locked in battle.[71]

Negative Information Policies and Practices: How and Why?

It is, of course, hardly surprising that in a society where the practice of public relations has become pervasive, the largest, perhaps most complex organization within the federal government relies on a broad range of PR activities as it scrambles every year to keep or increase its huge wedge of the budgetary pie. That such a public relations effort may be unduly propagandistic should be of deep concern to a democratic political system particularly when the propaganda is employed by the department that manages violence on the largest scale ever known to mankind.

Similarly, in the matter of restricting information, an organization aggressively "selling" itself may find it irresistible to use the secrecy stamp and the national security shield to hide information that harms its image.

Such sweeping analysis aside, various specific organizational explanations have been offered, some very appealing, to shed light on Pentagon manipulation of the facts. It has been said that the very nature of the military profession—authoritarian and therefore secretive—eliminates the possibility of official candor. Others argue that public relations men, whether in mufti or in uniform, have a vested interest in suppressing any information that reflects poorly on their organization. Consequently, an organization with as many PR men and women as the Pentagon has will put out little but selfserving information. A third explanation dismisses reported information manipulation as exaggeration. The Pentagon, it is argued, could rarely get away with such blatant news suppression since its every move is scrutinized constantly by a legion of aggressive journalists.

These, as well as other explanations of the Pentagon's negative information practices may all be accurate. Then, again, they may all miss the mark.

3

The Pentagon,
the Press
and Bad News

Just a few steps from one of the two wide pedestrian ramps that lead to the Mall entrance of the Pentagon lies a small parking lot. With its three dozen or so spaces, it is dwarfed by the building's north and south parking areas, parts of which are so remote a shuttle bus hauls the commuters to and fro. Even generals have to trudge hundreds of feet past the small lot to get to their coveted "nearby" parking spaces.

Half-empty much of the time, the small parking area is mostly reserved for a special group: the press.

From the lot it is a quick, 30-second walk to the tall but narrow wooden doors of the Mall entrance. Behind it a security guard checks everybody for building passes; visitors must wait here until an escort arrives to take them to their destination.

Reporters who cover the Pentagon on a regular basis flick out the pass issued by the Defense Department and automatically turn left into the E-ring Corridor as the guard routinely nods his go-ahead. After a couple of hundred steps, the width of the hallway shrinks by more than half. Large letters above the narrower section proclaim it as the "Correspondents Corridor." To the left of this corridor stands an open shrinclike area—a small, carpeted room decorated in gold and beige. Two open entrances offer access to the room, and the logogram journalists traditionally use to indicate the end of a story is embossed on the wall above those entrances: "-30-." Inside, directly between the entrances, an honor roll of war correspondents killed since the beginning of World War II is on display. Two large brass plaques hang on the far walls. The Defense Department's five "public information principles" appear on one plaque; on the other, the Freedom of Information Act.

Past that room, along both sides of the Correspondents Corridor, behind door after door, the center of the U.S. government's single largest public information apparatus is located.

The Pentagon Spokesman and His Domain

In the office of the assistant secretary of defense for public affairs sits the official who, along with his two top assistants, is the ubiquitous "Pentagon spokesman"—the assistant secretary for public affairs. He oversees a public relations network as farflung as American military installations and activities.

To guide him in this task, recent secretaries of defense have, as a routine part of being sworn in, issued sets of ringing public information principles. Hardly varying from secretary to secretary, they express a desire for a fully informed American public, a desire exceeded only by their concern for the security of the nation and the safety of its sailors, soldiers, and airmen. The principles reiterate that nothing is to be classified merely because its disclosure might cause the department to be criticized: all defense personnel are to abide by the Freedom of Information Act, in letter and in spirit; the department "has a responsibility to make available accurate and timely information" about what it is doing, and, consequently, when "interested citizens request information and/or speakers, every reasonable effort should be made to be responsive."

Using less sweeping language, other directives indicate how

the assistant secretary is to implement these principles. He is the one who sets defense policy on public affairs matters, particularly those that are of national or international significance. He is authorized to deal directly with the major commands of the Defense Department on public affairs problems, and all major components of the department "shall secure" advice from him before doing anything that has "significant public affairs implications."[1]

One brief paragraph in these directives sums up the post–World War II phenomenon of centralizing control over Pentagon public information activities at the highest level of the department. It specifies that the office of the assistant secretary for public affairs is to act "as the sole [Defense] agency at the Seat of Government for the release of official information through any form of public information media."

Toward that end, it is the assistant secretary's responsibility to ensure that all releasable material is screened so that nothing will be divulged that violates national security as defined by executive order. He is also to make sure that "official speeches, press releases, photographs, films and other information originated with the [Defense Department] for public release" are reviewed to "see whether such material is in conflict with established policies or programs" of the Pentagon or the administration generally.

Another directive spells out precisely what information has to be cleared at the very top of the Pentagon: material of national interest; matters that either originate or are to be released in Washington; "information concerning potential controversy among the military services"; matters that involve other federal agencies; information that deals with new or special weapons in the nuclear, chemical, and biological areas; anything else that "may be questionable from a security and policy standpoint." To top off the list, "other information specifically designated from time to time" by the Pentagon public information chief may also have to be cleared before it can be divulged. Specifying that all material covered must be released only after "it has been reviewed for security and conflict with [Defense Department]

and Government policies and programs," the directive further
states that its restrictions shall not be used to withhold information because "its release might tend to reveal administrative
error or inefficiency."[2]

At least on paper, then, the assistant secretary for public
affairs has extensive authority over the flow of newsworthy
information, including the ultimate authority of clearing or not
clearing virtually anything for release to the press. But what
about the other side of the coin? What role is he to play in
making available to the public information held by the Defense
Department?

Until the Freedom of Information Act was amended in 1975
top Pentagon officials were not required to get involved when
a lower official somewhere in the department decided to deny
a request for information from the public. According to directives then in force, the "initial determination" of whether to
make a requested record available could be made "at any suitable level and by any suitable official designated by the component. . . ." Such officials were advised—but not required—to
consult a public information officer if the request involved
"newsworthy" material or if it came "from news media representatives." If the request was denied, the requestor could then
appeal to the "head of the component having jurisdiction of the
record involved." If he denied the appeal, he was expected to
keep the Defense Department's general counsel informed.[3]

In the three services, a similar situation prevailed. Public
information specialists played insignificant roles in handling
requests for records made under the Freedom of Information
Act. Such requests usually were handled by records management personnel and, when the need arose, by legal or security-
classification experts. Only when a request involved "newsworthy matters" or came from a journalist was it recommended
that a public information specialist be consulted.[4]

With the tougher requirements of the amended act the assistant secretary for public affairs has been assigned a somewhat
more significant role, at least on paper. He is to "direct and
administer" a "freedom of information program" for the De-

fense Department. Everyone in the department is now required to advise the assistant secretary's office "of cases of public interest, particularly those on appeal, when the issues raised are unusual, precedent setting, matters of disagreement among components . . ." or when the denial of a request may result in "news media interest."

However, the initial decision to deny or not to deny a record still "may be made at any suitable level and by any suitable official designated by the component. . . ." Furthermore, the official picked to handle freedom-of-information matters "should"—but doesn't have to—touch bases with the local public information officer to advise him of requests from the press or to receive help with newsworthy material.

More important, the new directive still specifies that, as in the past, the last word on whether to release a record does not come from the assistant secretary for public affairs. It is still spoken by "the head of the component having jurisdiction, or by his designee . . ."[5]—in other words, by nearly anyone.

Getting the Word
and Spreading It

Almost every morning the secretary of defense meets with a dozen of his key aides to be briefed on the latest crisis and the daily agenda of government and congressional events. At these meetings the secretary tells the "Pentagon spokesman" what position to take at the next scheduled press briefing. If a new issue is involved, the secretary and his aides decide which defense components or officials to consult for further facts. While information is being gathered, an interim announcement may be made stating that the problem is being pursued, and press queries will be answered as soon as the facts are available.

Senior public affairs officials attend these meetings not only to find out what the secretary of defense wants to say on a particular issue but also to be fully informed about all major matters involving the department, including its innermost secrets. Almost everything that the secretary deals with, argues one former assistant secretary for public affairs, must also be known by his public spokesman. That need to know is "nearly total." Indeed, the more sensitive and secret the issue is, "the more important that he be aware of it so that he can help safeguard the information in his worldwide formulation of public affairs policy."[6]

To ensure that the assistant secretary for public affairs and his two senior deputies have access to all information, no matter how highly classified, they "carry some exotic clearances" said one senior public affairs specialist—including some clearances so secret that he didn't know they existed until he joined the staff.

The Pentagon's chief public information official, in turn, oversees three directorates that help him implement the department's public affairs policies—community relations, defense information, and security review.

The Defense Information Directorate is the primary funnel through which defense information is channeled to the public via the news media. Subdivided into a press and audiovisual division, the directorate, as one recent assistant secretary for public affairs described its role, "issues all of our news releases —printed, film, audio. It arranges appointments and interviews for newsmen and answers their queries. It provides authors and publishers with assistance as requested."[7]

The information directorate is in business seven days a week, 24 hours a day. Its main office area resembles the city room of a medium-sized newspaper. Phones ring, typewriters clang, and almost everybody wears civilian clothes, making it difficult to distinguish public affairs officers from the Pentagon correspondents who occasionally walk through.

Setting the directorate's main office area apart from a city room, however, are the pictures of planes and warships, the maps of various parts of the world, the clocks giving local time and the hour in Peking, Honolulu, Greenwich, and Moscow, and the red tags on filing cabinets reminding their custodian that they are "open."

Since the end of the Vietnam War, the directorate is less busy, its operations less hectic. During one year late in the war, for example, it answered 45,000 new queries, issued 868 news releases and provided correspondents with another 600 informal memoranda on various issues, arranged 850 interviews, handled 35 news conferences involving the secretary of defense plus another 33 informal meetings he had with reporters, filled 752 requests for news photographs, made 131 newsfilm releases, provided assistance on 156 motion picture productions, and on and on.

Since then, the press briefings that used to be held daily only take place twice or three times a week. Unless a crisis has erupted, such as a flare-up in the Middle East, only 12 to 15 correspondents attend. Indeed, two dozen jobs were eliminated in the press division when the American involvement in Southeast Asia subsided.

The Directorate of Security Review is the other crucial component in the assistant secretary's domain critical to the flow of information from the Department of Defense to the public. The Pentagon's top public relations man monitors all information through this directorate to ensure that its release will neither violate national security nor contradict the established policies of the department or the White House.

The directorate's out-of-the-way entrance is studded with signs proclaiming it a restricted area, accessible to authorized personnel only. In contrast to the hustle and bustle of the press division's office area, the atmosphere inside the security review office brings to mind a reference library. Bookshelves line the walls, banks of filing cabinets occupy much floor space; in various offices analysts quietly pore over stacks of papers. During the course of a year, the staff of about 30 handles approximately 180,000 pages of congressional and noncongressional material,[8] the former ostensibly only for security, the latter for security as well as policy.

Despite the ivory-tower ambience that pervades the security and policy review office area, this directorate, as the next chapter will show, is at least as critical to the handling of public information as the press division.*

Three Variations on
the Same Theme

The office of the assistant secretary of defense for public affairs is the most visible aspect of the department's public information machinery, but certainly not the only one. Tucked away in different parts of the Pentagon are the headquarters that guide the worldwide public relations activities of the army, navy, and air force.

In their essentials the public affairs programs of the three services are very similar.[9] For instance, heading the army's PR activities is a major general, the chief of information. His naval counterpart has the same title but is a rear admiral; his colleague in the air force is also a major general, but his title is director of information. Each wears two hats: each advises the civilian head of his service, the secretary, as well as his uniformed boss, a four-star general or admiral, on public relations matters. In addition to answering directly to the top officials of his own service, each is also the key link between his branch of the armed forces and the assistant secretary of defense for public affairs.

Although army, navy, and air force information offices may differ in organizational detail, each seeks to inform the public about its service, mainly through the mass media. Thus, there may be a news desk to process press inquiries as they pour in daily from coast to coast, a branch to assist writers exploring a topic for a book or magazine article, or a section that specializes in solving pictorial or broadcast problems the media encounter

---

*The third directorate, that for community relations, is primarily concerned with building "good relations" between Defense and the general public as well as such special publics as business, labor, etc., emphasizing channels other than the mass media.

in covering Defense affairs. To assist in the distribution of routine news items, each service has a special center—located in various places around the country—that daily churns out hundreds of releases about military personnel and mails them to scores of local radio and television stations and hometown newspapers. Each service also has major branch offices outside of Washington. Their number and location have fluctuated over the years, but all continue to have branches on both coasts—the West Coast branches working with the motion picture industry, the East Coast branches with the national media headquartered in New York City.

The chief of information of each service directly controls these field offices. But there are, of course, dozens of additional public information officers—or public affairs officers, as the navy prefers to call them—stationed at military installations around the world. The information officer in the field is not under the immediate control of his service's chief of information. He can solicit his advice and consider the guidance provided from the Pentagon, but he must carry out the directives and obey the orders of his commanding officer in the field.

On the other hand, when deciding what type of information is releasable, the public information specialist in the field must follow the policies set by the Pentagon and the office of the Assistant secretary of defense for public affairs. Army units, for example, are put on notice that information "in any form concerning the overall plans, policies, programs, or operations" of the Defense Department, the army, or the federal government "is normally released at the seat of Government by the Department of Defense." Field commanders are only allowed to release material "to local media which is wholly within the mission and scope of their command."[10] As the navy puts it: "If in doubt, submit it."[11]

Whether submitted to Washington or not, all material is subject to security and policy review by each service prior to release. In the army, for instance, material for use in the "nationally circulated media" has to be forwarded to the office of the chief of information to be reviewed for "security, policy, accuracy and propriety." Here the review function is handled—ironically enough—mainly by the Office for the Freedom of Information. Despite its name, it mainly censors material for policy, accuracy, and propriety. Questions involving security classification are referred to intelligence experts. If the matter is of national significance, the corps of security- and policy-review analysts working for the assistant secretary of defense for public affairs has the last word on whether the material violates security or conforms with established policies and programs.[12]

Pentagon Channels for
Disseminating the News

Once every week or two all spaces in the Pentagon's press parking lot are taken; cars even spill over on the grass. The sound and camera crews usually arrive early to set up their equipment in the press briefing room.

The television crews set up their cameras in the rear, atop two platforms, allowing them a clear shot over the four rows of gray folding chairs directly in front of the speaker's podium. Sound technicians run cables to the lectern bearing the seal of the Department of Defense; other workers take readings with light meters in front of the blue curtain that serves as a backdrop. An army sergeant drops pieces of paper on the folding chairs, reserving seats for the New York *Times,* CBS News, the *Wall Street Journal,* and so on. Another section of folding chairs, to the left of the podium, is reserved for Pentagon officials.

As the appointed hour nears, the room begins to fill. Without announcement, the assistant secretary of defense for public affairs appears, followed by the secretary of defense. The reporters take their seats and, as the room settles down, the secretary of defense leans on the lectern and opens the press conference with a brief statement, usually on a current area of interest.

After a few minutes, he begins taking questions from the reporters. Unlike presidential press conferences, the pace is leisurely. No one jumps up to be recognized. The secretary eventually gets around to every raised hand. Reporters can pursue with follow-up questions. Indeed, the pace is often such that several reporters can ask a series of questions.

After 45 minutes or so, the number of raised hands decreases, and the assistant secretary for public affairs announces that only two more questions will be taken. Those answered, he adjourns the press conference.

During the conference, a number of public affairs officers follow it over small loudspeakers that carry what is said into their offices and those of several senior officials elsewhere in the Pentagon, the State Department, and even the White House. Several hours after each conference a complete transcript is made available to officials.

This process represents one of the primary channels the Pentagon employs to provide information to the public. It is used not only by the secretary of defense but by all senior officials. One day it may be the secretary of the army discussing the all-volunteer army; on another, the chairman of the Joint Chiefs of Staff describing a new major weapons system. Most of the time, however, the assistant secretary for public affairs or one of his deputies is at the microphones.

The pace and tone of these briefings vary considerably depending on the sensitivity of the issues involved. Former Assistant Secretary of Defense for Public Affairs Jerry W. Friedheim, for example, sometimes would get "around questions by pleading ignorance or by being brief, and sometimes [by using] them to criticize the enemy."[13]

The answers reporters receive can depend on asking precisely the right questions, which apparently does not help Pentagon-press relations. For example:

Q. *Did you confirm yesterday Iran's purchase of F-14's?*
A. We weren't asked yesterday.

Q. *Then I'm asking today.*
A. Yes, the government of Iran has decided to purchase an additional 50 F-14's, to make the total purchase agreed

upon to date 80. We're not going into details of price and
delivery. We are referring questions on those matters to
the government of Iran. Published reports have been in
the approximate ballpark.

Q. *I wonder why it's necessary to play 20 questions with you
people on something like this. Grumman has put out the
word in New York and it was in several publications under
New York dateline, obviously from that source. You had a
piece of paper prepared and General James had it yesterday, waiting for the appropriate question. Why didn't you
simply just come out and say it?*

A. In the case of foreign military sales, we try to respect the
wishes of the foreign government involved.

Q. *Grumman didn't. Grumman was putting the thing out. I
don't think there was any reason . . .*

A. You asked about the Department of Defense, not Grumman. I can't speak for Grumman. I can speak for Defense,
and we try to respect the wishes of the government involved.

Q. *Is there anything else that you're waiting with a prepared
answer that if we get the right question you'll have it?*

A. We do try to prepare answers to questions that might
come up, yes. That's a regular part of the operation of this
office.

Q. *Sometimes your Department likes to get things out, but they
don't want to be in the position of announcing it, so if
somebody happens to think of the right question they have
the answer. Is there something there you'd like to tell us?*

A. No . . .[14]

And the topics covered at the briefings range widely:

Q. *Do Army counterintelligence officers have a policeman's
right to inspect the credentials of reporters inside this building?*

A. What were the circumstances? It's not an academic question. . . .

Q. *It certainly isn't.*

A. If you explain the circumstances, I'll try to address it.

Q. *The other day an Army counterintelligence officer demanded to see my building pass.*

A. During normal working hours?

Q. *During normal working hours and in a public corridor of the Pentagon. I'm perfectly willing to show them to policemen, but I don't want counterintelligence people going through my billfold.*

A. We'll try to find out what their authority is in a case of that kind.

Q. [*Mr. Fred Hoffman of the Associated Press*] *Were you coming out of the ladies' room?**

A. [Mr. John Finney of the New York *Times*] No. A group of reporters were standing outside the Secretary of Defense's office in the corridor waiting for Mr. Dayan and a young counterintelligence officer came up and demanded to see our building passes and I think that may be overstepping his authority.

A. [Mr. William Beecher, deputy assistant secretary of defense for public affairs] When you have a foreign official visiting, sometimes in the effort to provide security, people involved in security will check out everybody that they think looks suspicious. Did you look suspicious, John?

Mr. Finney: I probably did, and maybe I'm making too much of this except I am rather fearful of Army counterintelligence on the basis of some of their past escapades. And, it seems to me that that function of security and checking

---

*The question refers to an explosion that was set off in a women's restroom in the Pentagon during the height of anti-Vietnam war demonstrations.

on building passes should be reserved to the Pentagon police.

A. In a special case where they're trying to provide security for—in this case it was General Dayan—and there was a crowd of people outside the Secretary's office . . .

Mr. Finney: Not a crowd, a gathering.

A. OK, a gathering of people. I don't mean to make light of it; it's something more understandable. I just thought you were walking through the corridor and suddenly someone stopped you and asked to see your identification.

Mr. Finney: No, but that would be the next step for them.

A. We'll look into what their authority is, John, and we'll inform you.

Q. *What is their authority? They used to come around the press room at night years ago and demand to see building passes, and it always kind of amused me when they found out I didn't have one because they were trainees and they didn't know what to do next. I've never quite understood what the CID's (Criminal Investigations Division) got to do with this GSA (General Services Administration) building.*

A. It's open to the public. But since that explosion in the women's lavatory, as you know, the public doesn't have free access. They have to identify themselves coming in. Passes are required . . .[15]

The press release or handout is another routine channel for relaying information.[16] The Pentagon cranks out about 1,000 "blue tops"—Defense Department jargon for its press releases because of their two-inch wide, electric-blue heading—in the course of a year. In addition, scores of films and photos are released to the media in Washington, as well as hundreds of other releases made by Defense components around the country.

Another major channel for the flow of information from the Pentagon to the press is the interview. Hundreds are officially set up each year by the office of the assistant secretary for public affairs. Many more are arranged by the individual military services or unofficially initiated by journalists.

Answering inquiries from the media constitutes a fourth major channel of information. The Defense information directorate in one recent year alone handled more than 40,000 such queries. In addition, the army, navy, and air force on their own annually respond to an uncounted number of less significant queries.

Although sometimes overlooked as a channel between reporters and officials, the news query is important not only because it is used by Washington correspondents but because for many newspapers, magazines, freelance writers, and radio and television stations around the country, it is the only way of eliciting information from the Pentagon.

Another important channel for transmitting Defense information to the public—and often vital to correspondents covering the department—is testimony given before congressional committees by both top-echelon and lesser Pentagon officials. Although many of these hearings take place behind closed doors, the censored transcripts still provide much detailed data. Speeches and articles written by Defense officials are still another information source, though they rarely provide as much substantive material as congressional transcripts.

Informal channels include the background briefing. It may be conducted by an information officer or by a senior official who invites one or several carefully selected journalists to a meeting. The rules governing "backgrounders" vary. In some cases the press and the official agree that nothing can be used; sometimes the matters discussed may be releasable but without attribution; at other times a delay may be involved before the material may be made public.[17]

The other major informal channel is the leak. It differs significantly from the backgrounder. Usually it involves only one official dealing with a single reporter who is given the information exclusively with the proviso that it can be used only without linking it in any way to its source.[18] The news leak occurs for a variety of reasons—to derail a government policy with which an official disagrees, to boost a policy he advocates, to right what he considers a wrong—and Pentagon officials have employed it at least as frequently as others in Washington.

Indeed, leaks spring with some regularity when the Defense Department budget is before Congress. Known among reporters as the "threat leak," it "is the annual leak by the Pentagon that the Soviet Union is on the march, generally with military hardware." Or it is used by one military service against the other. In the words of one former Pentagon official: "There will be a report that a particular Army missile isn't working properly. This is usually a Navy leak because the Navy wants more money for its missiles. . . . If you want to find out what's wrong with aircraft carriers, talk to someone in the Air Force; he'll leak all the secret data you need."[19]

Some Pentagon leaks have spawned major news stories. For example, a tip from a source with Defense Department connections led to Seymour Hersh's exposé of the My Lai massacre.[20] Indeed, Hersh's subsequent disclosure that the army's official investigation of the My Lai incident discovered another massacre and promptly covered it up was made possible by an anonymous Pentagon official who supplied Hersh with photo copies of the panel's full report, several thousand pages in length and labeled, "for official use only."[21]

The Correspondents
at the Pentagon

At the receiving end of the Defense Department's various news dissemination channels are, of course, the journalists who cover the department. Of late, according to a Defense Department list, there are 37 "Pentagon press correspondents"—the "regulars" who cover the Department on a full-time or fairly routine basis—and 20 other "defense correspondents" who are to be called whenever a significant issue arises.

They work out of a large room directly across the Correspondents Corridor from the Directorate for Defense Information. Painted light green, with six large, curtainless windows overlooking the lawn surrounding the Pentagon, the media's headquarters at the Pentagon always looks slightly disheveled and even bears a few signs of modest irreverence.

The tops of rust-specked, olive-green filing cabinets are piled high with congressional reports, other documents, some old magazines, and a scattering of blue tops. Some of the cluttered desks are separated by partitions that hold yellowing maps of Southeast Asia, a buxom pin-up or two, and a few slogans: "War may be Hell, but it's a fine time to test weapons."

Much of the time there is little activity in the press room. Two or three men, usually in shirtsleeves, sit at typewriters or talk on the phone. More often than not, the correspondents of United Press International and the Associated Press are on hand. One of the television network's representatives may be in a special section of the room outfitted for making audio reports via the telephone. The room becomes busy only when a crisis arises somewhere or if a major press conference is scheduled. But even then its capacity is not taxed.

One reason for the sparse occupancy is that there are far fewer than 37 regulars at the Pentagon, its list of correspondents notwithstanding. Considering the department's vital role in U.S. national security policy formulation and execution, its $120 billion-a-year budget, and its personnel of some 3 million men and women stationed around the world, the number of regulars with a Pentagon beat is surprisingly small: 10 to 12 full-time correspondents representing the general circulation media. When the correspondents of special publications—for example, trade journals and newspapers aimed solely at military and other special audiences—are included, there are still only about 20.[22]

How do these 20 correspondents cover the Department of Defense? One of the veterans among the regulars, Charles Corrdry, who has reported on the Pentagon since 1953—first for UPI, since then for the Baltimore *Sun*—feels that today hand-outs are seldom very helpful. Until the end of the Eisenhower administration the press releases used to contain considerable newsworthy material because the military services were more independent in handling their PR. With the subsequent centralization of information activities in the office of the secretary of defense, handouts, as well as the public information officers who write them, have become useful only for obtaining routine information.

Corrdry also finds official briefings and backgrounders of little use except when a major event is involved. Nor do texts of speeches "contain much any more from a news standpoint." And submitting queries is of limited use because the answers elicited "are not very helpful. The reporter who relies on them is not a very good reporter."

To cover the Pentagon well, the reporter must develop his own sources with a discerning eye. Corrdry finds, for instance, that the civilian secretaries of the military service have lost their importance as news sources because they are no longer in the military chain of command (which runs from the secretary of defense through the Joint Chief of Staff to the commanders of eight field commands). To emphasize his point, he recalls that during the 1970 invasion of Cambodia he discovered that the secretary of the air force did not know of the invasion until it was under way.

Consequently, he feels that key military officials are more important to the reporter—the chairman of the Joint Chiefs of Staff, officials in the office of the Joint Chiefs, the chiefs of staff of the army and air force, and the chief of naval operations. Sources within each service are also critical, primarily on purely military matters, because their tendency to overstate their position serves as a counterbalance to the other services and the office of the secretary of defense. But Corrdry finds these service sources of limited usefulness because if they say something important on the record, they must go through the assistant secretary of defense for public affairs.

He also advocates that a reporter stake out areas of concentration within the department to gain an overall understanding of the national defense situation. In his case, he zeroes in on the budget. "If you know what's happening to the money—well, that's one sound way to cover the military." The comptroller's office is therefore his key to covering the Pentagon on a day-in, day-out basis. "They know their own bailiwick and everybody else's." Moreover, a variety of specialists work in that office. "They are real wizards. They've been there a long time." Most are career officials who will remain on hand when military officers are transferred. And perhaps most important for the reporter, "they are competent and are willing to talk to you because they know what they can and can't say."

Others echoed much of what Corrdry said. Fred Hoffman, Associated Press correspondent at the Pentagon for 15 years, was particularly emphatic about the importance of meticulously cultivating sources. They are critical to covering the department, "particularly when things get hot." To buttress his point, he recalled that when the 1973 war in the Middle East broke out, "the government was making a great effort to keep the lid on." There were no briefings, no handouts. The former assistant secretary for public affairs, Jerry Friedheim, "shut everything down." Within a few hours, however, Hoffman had learned that U.S. forces were placed on alert. In another hour and a half he found out that the army and air force had assembled their battle staffs and emergency personnel. Sources carefully nurtured over the years were crucial. "You don't get that kind of information by being here a month."

Richard Levine of the *Wall Street Journal* and Michael Getler of the Washington *Post,* who were covering the Pentagon on a full-time basis for their papers when interviewed, agree that a network of sources is important. But they stressed sources outside of the Pentagon—in the Congress, the State Department, and other agencies that play a significant part in the making of national defense policy.

Like Corrdry, Levine, and Getler, Bob Schieffer, who was in his fourth year of covering the Pentagon for CBS News when interviewed, also stressed the complexity of reporting Defense news. It requires a constant effort to remain abreast of such subjects as military hardware, foreign policy, research and development, military history, military sociology, tactics and strategy, and the budgetary process. One way to do that is to stay on top of congressional testimony. As Thomas Steinhauser, executive editor of the *Armed Forces Journal International,* sees it, that testimony contains extensive, detailed information that not only saves asking a lot of basic questions but provides a good check on what emerges from interviews with Defense officials.

None of the correspondents interviewed thought he could do an adequate job by relying primarily on official information channels. Indeed, only one, Dana Schmidt, who had covered the Pentagon on a part-time basis for the *Christian Science Monitor,* indicated that press briefings, handouts, and answers to queries are of more than secondary importance. For him they are "a point of departure" because "they suggest the unknown." After that, he said, queries placed with information officers may provide answers, as may interviews arranged at his request. But he also said that his best Defense stories have come from his own sources on Capitol Hill, embassy row, the State Department, and elsewhere.

On one crucial aspect of covering the Defense Department there was complete agreement: none of the interviewed journalists did much traveling in connection with reporting Defense affairs. It is rare for them to leave town to see at first hand what the U.S. military does around the world.

The Handling of Bad News:
Reporters versus Officials

This is the setting, then, in which bad news about the Pentagon is handled.

But do the journalists and officials involved in the handling of Defense information agree that some Pentagon officials withhold or distort negative, newsworthy, releasable information? And, if so, how?

In general terms, the journalists' descriptions of how they cover the Pentagon suggest that they don't think officials go very

far in making information available. All the interviewed correspondents—among whom were eight of the ten to twelve who
cover Defense on a regular, full-time basis for the general
media* agreed that the Pentagon puts out a great deal of information but usually does not volunteer bad news.

Not all Defense officials† who handle news concede the point.
For example, the army and air force chiefs of information and
the navy's deputy chief of information—who said he spoke for
his boss—all said that generally all information that is newsworthy and needed by the public to be fully informed is made
available.

But a top official from the office of the assistant secretary of
defense didn't feel as strongly about the matter. He thought it
unrealistic not to expect that officials will at times attempt to
make themselves or a particular situation look as good as possible, and equally unrealistic to expect them to *volunteer* negative,
sensitive information.

A few, however, saw the situation very differently. Cmdr.
Jack M. White, director of program planning for the navy's
chief of information and a career public affairs officer, agreed
that things are changing, but at present "the system is not tuned
to coughing up sensitive information." Indeed, when pressed for
specifics, most of the officials agreed that attempts are made to
withhold or at least play down bad news. The chief of the news
branch of the army's Public Information Division, Lt. Col.
Leonard F. B. Reed, Jr., pointed to the handling of the My Lai
incident. "If it happens, that's how it happens." The chief of the
air force's Public Information Division Col. Robert Hermann,
said those in the air force who don't understand how the American media work distort or withhold information. "You may not

---

*In addition to these eight regulars, one journalist who covered the
Pentagon on a part-time basis for the general media and another who
works for a service-oriented journal were interviewed in summer 1974.

†Twenty-three officials regularly involved in the handling of public
information matters were interviewed during the main data-gathering
effort for this study in 1974–75.

believe this, but there are people who believe everything that appears in the paper has been released by an IO [Information Officer] or that the press uses our releases verbatim." He added, "It happens from the sincere belief that it's in the best interest of the country. . . . But there's also the guy who knows exactly what he's doing."

A senior career public affairs officer in the navy, who asked to be anonymous, agreed. He said that in cases where there is no legitimate reason for withholding the negative information, the usual practice is simply not to tell all in a public announcement. "It is held back and provided only if we're asked."

Another officer in the office of the navy's chief of information echoed those views. Negative, unrestricted news is manipulated "mainly by way of telling only part of the story or by overemphasizing the good part."

Similar tactics were described by the chief of the Public Information Division in the office of the army's chief of information. "No institution," said Col. Rolf Utegaard, "makes available all adverse information about itself, at least not right away. And that includes the army." Normally, if a critical situation arises, it is investigated and an attempt is made to begin corrective action before the news is released. But if a query comes up before the army plans to make the information public, it is usually released only if the reporter asks precisely the correct question and, naturally, if it is legally releasable.

But what if the questions are not precisely correct? The colonel shrugged his shoulders and raised his eyebrows. He eventually acknowledged that the reporter would get the right answers only if he asked the right questions.

A definite pattern emerges from these officials' answers. Extremely sensitive information—such as the U.S. mining of Haiphong harbor—will be withheld for only a limited time. Eventually a leak will spring if the matter is significant enough. Negative, unrestricted information may be withheld for longer periods of time if the matter does not seem susceptible to leaks.

Generally, however, bad news—whether its release is initiated by a Defense component or a leak—will be manipulated in some way. Important elements of a story may be omitted; its importance may be obfuscated by overemphasizing the positive aspects of the matter; answers to press queries may be unduly delayed or so completely bland as to convey no information at all.

Not all the officials, however, agree that bad news is manipulated. Brig. Gen. Joseph F. Cutrona, at the time director of defense information for the assistant secretary of defense for public affairs, was one of four who said that either manipulation does not occur or that it no longer happens. Stressing that he has never seen news management take place, the army general said that newsworthy information may occasionally be held up inadvertently or delayed intentionally but only if timing is critical, as for example, in the case of a contract award whose announcement is delayed until after the stock market closes for the day. Asked to explain the handling of information about the 1968 My Lai incident and, particularly, the misleading announcement out of Fort Benning of the charges against Calley, the general said that was a military justice matter, handled by the particular service involved.*

The air force's director of information, Maj. Gen. Guy E. Hairston, also said he didn't know of any cases of withholding or distortion of newsworthy information. At first he snapped, "You wouldn't be human without that instinct." But then the general—who became director only two weeks before the interview and whose only other public affairs duty during more than three decades in the military had been nine months as the air force's deputy director of information—leaned back and paused for some moments: "Well, you know human beings have their failings, but I'll be damned if I know of any cases."

The reporters, on the other hand, were unanimous on the

---

*From August 1968 to August 1969, General Cutrona was the special assistant for Southeast Asia in the office of the assistant secretary of defense for public affairs; from September 1969 to August 1970 he was chief of information for the U.S. Military Assistance Command in Vietnam.

subject of the Pentagon's attempts at news manipulation.† All
concurred with Corrdry of the Baltimore *Sun,* who said such
manipulation is a constant problem for the Washington press in
general. At the Defense Department, he added, "The hotter, the
more important the event, the more difficult it is to get information when you want it."

Another Defense correspondent felt that with the end of U.S.
involvement in Vietnam, such activity "on the surface, is less.
But if we had a crisis they'd go back to the old withholding and
manipulation tactics." These tactics are still in use, he said,
though in less sensational ways than during the height of the
war. He pointed to the devious way information concerning a
$1-billion military equipment stockpile for Southeast Asia was
handled early in 1974.[23]

One of the most senior Pentagon reporters, who knew the late
General Creighton Abrams well, recalled discussing the problem of information manipulation with Abrams at a social function. "You guys don't know the half of it," the former commander of U.S. troops in Vietnam told him.

The correspondents pointed to a variety of examples and
catalogued a list of practices they have encountered to buttress
their claim of the continuing pervasiveness of information manipulation. They agreed with the public affairs officials that, in
highly sensitive matters, the Pentagon may simply withhold all
information. "The lid goes on," was the way Corrdry put it.
Suddenly knowledgeable officials become unavailable or silent.

---

†It should be noted that there is close agreement between the kind
of information journalists as well as officials consider bad news. Both
groups were asked to cite examples of such information. Both mentioned cost overruns, domestic army intelligence activities, oil spills,
race and drug problems, the My Lai incident—cited most frequently
by both—problems with the all-volunteer army, incidents involving
chemical and biological weapons, lack of integrity by Defense personnel. As one colonel described bad news: "Anything that creates a bad
image of the services." Said a newsman: "Anything that'll have negative impact on the Pentagon."

Corrdry and five other correspondents recalled the way information connected with the 1972 mining of Haiphong harbor was handled. After Nixon announced the mining, the *Wall Street Journal* asked Richard Levine to write a story on mining operations in general. "Suddenly the lid went on as far as mining goes—no matter where or how," Levine said.

Aside from the outright refusal to provide information—either by "putting the lid on" or by claiming that it is classified —the journalists cited delay as a major problem. When it comes to unfavorable but unrestricted information, said Schieffer of CBS News, "you have to drag it out of them." Although some public information officials try to help pry information loose— for instance, by getting it declassified—the usual procedure is for bad news to be "delayed again and again." Or as Joe Kane of *Time* put it, "If it suits their purposes, they'll get it out that afternoon. If not, it may come out some day or never."

Unresponsiveness was another major problem area the correspondents mentioned. Kane said he found that submitting queries involving sensitive information was nearly useless. He maintained, "It doesn't matter whether my question is answered but whether the form is filled out."

John Finney of the New York *Times* was less harsh. Many public information officers, he found, feel a great responsibility to respond fully and accurately, but in practice they have to come back with what "the lowest bureaucratic denominator permits." And, he added, the "inertia of the bureaucracy provides information of limited use."

Steinhauser of the *Armed Forces Journal* pointed out that information officials usually will answer only what is asked. Little or nothing is volunteered; few attempts are made to provide a complete picture.

Such tactics are not limited to the handling of queries. Levine of the *Journal* said that news releases involving bad news can sometimes be nearly undecipherable. He cited a blue top issued in connection with an unsuccessful helicopter project whose development costs had been very high. When it was decided to terminate the project, a release was issued. "On the afternoon it happened, a one-paragraph release came out—without background, without help," said Levine. "It was in the system's interest to play down the bad." Such practices, he said, are not as much of a problem for reporters like himself who spend all of their time on Defense affairs. But those who cover the Defense Department on a part-time basis as part of their Washington beat do not know the exact context into which that one paragraph fits.

A less effective tactic, but one several reporters mentioned, is the curtailing of access to officials. That knowledgeable general or that well-informed assistant secretary simply will not be available to reporters.

A related practice, monitoring interviews, was a cause of much friction during the 1960s, when it was pervasive. Today Pentagon correspondents no longer see it as a significant block in the flow of information. But another questionable custom of the 1960s lives on: investigations to find the anonymous sources of stories.

4

A Matter of Policy

~~~~~~~~~~~~~~~~~~~~~~~~~~~~~

"Bad" news is withheld or distorted by Pentagon officials from time to time. There is no doubt about that; a variety of specific instances make it clear. So do journalists covering the Defense Department, and the public affairs specialists involved in handling unfavorable but releasable information. How it happens is equally clear: through delay, quibbling, obfuscation, misclassification, "putting on the lid," even outright lying.

But why?

To date, the responses to that question unfortunately involve more speculation than elucidation. By drawing on what's been written about large, complex bureaucracies, the media, and the military, it is possible, however, to single out some probable causes that appear promising as roadmarkers—not all of which, by design, point in the same direction—in the exploration of why defense officials handle "blackeye" stories as they do.

Consider the role policy considerations play in the processing of bad news. Officials involved in making policy decisions do not act in a vacuum. Instead, they belong to a huge, complicated public bureaucracy that must constantly interact with its envivironment, if only to obtain needed manpower and to safeguard its huge budget.

As a public organization competing with other agencies for limited resources, the Pentagon needs political backing in American society in general and among relevant interest groups in particular. That outside backing generates legislative and executive support for the department.

Compared to most other federal agencies, the department has generally displayed considerable dexterity since World War II in obtaining a disproportionate share of the available resources.[1] There are many reasons for this success—external threats to the nation, public, congressional, and presidential perception of those threats.[2] When compared with spending in such less visible, less tangible areas as health, education, and welfare, particularly on the state and local level, spending in the name of national security has usually come out ahead "whenever military needs pressed unusually hard" since the start of World War II.[3] And, judging by the effort Pentagon officials expend on it, they have found the PR tactic of promoting national security an effective weapon in the home-front conflict over resources. Through a steady flow of positive information, the Pentagon seeks a winning position in that conflict by continuously trying to broaden external support for national security. Conversely, it seems Pentagon officials can be expected to limit the flow of information that would hurt such support.[4]

In short, information is an important tool in Pentagon administrative politics. Thus, the question: Do defense officials withhold or distort bad news if they think it could adversely affect department policies and programs?

The Rise of Policy Review

During the past three decades, the Defense Department has become increasingly concerned with the ways in which policy-related information—that is, information about a course of action to which all or part of the military establishment has committed itself either by word or deed—is disseminated to the public.

On a formal basis, that concern can be traced back to 1949. In the process of consolidating the public information activities of the military services within the office of the secretary of defense, a security review branch was included in the new Office of Information. Its job was to clear material for reasons of both security and policy. Within four months, however, "public clamor, especially over the policy review practice," caused Defense Secretary James Forrestal to pull back and to limit review to security matters only.[5]

That situation lasted eight years. But indirectly the Security Review Branch kept a hand in policy review right along. For instance, in 1950, when President Harry S. Truman directed that the State Department review all speeches by executive branch officials for foreign policy implications, it became the job of the Security Review Branch to identify all such public statements by Defense personnel and to forward them to State for clearance. In 1951, it was given similar responsibility to coordinate with the Atomic Energy Commission all Defense Department publications dealing with atomic energy. In 1955, the office was officially "directed to *coordinate* the policy review operations of the Defense Department by 'flagging' information with policy connotations."

Finally, in 1957, policy review was once more formalized when the assistant secretary for public affairs was told to make sure that all Defense-originated material destined for publications was reviewed for agreement with the department's stated policies. In turn, the Directorate of Security Review was held responsible for policy review, thereby ending "an eight-year ban on the conduct of such operations by the review office."[6]

Shortly after the Kennedy administration took office, the directorate got into hot water—a situation adroit bureaucrats used to legitimize policy review. The issue was kicked off less than a month after the new administration entered office, when Robert S. McNamara asserted, "It's inappropriate for any member of the Defense Department to speak on the subject of foreign

policy."[7] In the heat of the cold war, a subcommittee of the
Senate Armed Forces Committee began hearings on charges of
"muzzling" and related issues. It wanted to know, for example,
why in one general's speech the word "victory" was changed to
"defeat of aggression."[8]

Eventually the committee went so far as to ask the assistant
security-review director to identify the analyst who had deleted
certain sections from a Defense official's statement prepared for
delivery before a congressional committee. He refused, on orders from McNamara. The secretary subsequently appeared
before the subcommittee, presenting a letter from President
Kennedy that invoked executive privilege in the matter.[9]

In time the subcommittee concluded that McNamara's original statement ". . . was far too broad and literally precluded all
discussion of foreign policy" because it "was not definite or
specific." However, the subcommittee also said:

> While [the statement] has not been formally modified, in
> actual practice its applications seem to have been clarified. It
> is now recognized that discussions of foreign policy matters
> are permissible provided they do not conflict with established
> foreign policy and provided they are cleared with, and ap-
> proved by, the Department of State.[10]

Although the subcommittee asked for various changes to
make the clearance process more consistent and less arbitrary,
its report was the "first clear, forceful endorsement" of the
practice from outside the Pentagon.[11]

In short, policy review could now be interpreted as being
sanctioned by Congress, as an excerpt from the Security Review
Directorate's "Indoctrination and Training Program," written
by its director, shows:

> I believe the best explanation of the need for this function [of
> policy review] is contained in a brief extract from a 1962
> report of the Special Preparedness Investigating Subcommit-
> tee of the Senate Committee on Armed Forces:

"The propriety of a responsible review system can be clearly bottomed upon the best interest and the welfare of the nation. It is unthinkable that the four military services should go divergent ways and contribute to the public confusion by speaking with diverse tongues upon our foreign or domestic policy and objectives. Irreparable harm can result if the thousands of military officers are free to express their own personal views in conflict with or dissent from the policies laid down by their Commander in Chief. . . .

"The urgency and necessity of the cold war itself requires that, with respect to established national and foreign policy, we speak with one tongue and not with a thousand."[12]

Thus, not withstanding the assertion by some that the Directorate for Security Review checks material only for breaches of military security classification,[13] the office concurrently checks for "conflicts with established policies or programs of the Department of Defense or of the national government."[14]

What information does it scrutinize? Potentially any "information and material from military or other sources intended for dissemination through all media of publication, . . . including Congressional testimony, book and magazine manuscripts, newspaper articles, news releases, advertisements, speeches, radio scripts and still and motion pictures."[15]

Today, the security review directorate is the final, most critical filter through which sensitive information must pass on its way to the public. However, to make sure nothing falls through the cracks, the military services back it up with their own security- and policy-review operations.

Each handles the review function somewhat differently, but regulations and manuals dealing with the release of information make it rather clear to army,[16] navy,[17] and air force personnel[18] —particularly to information officers—that policy considerations should be considered in the release of information. They all stress that information of national interest, originated in Washington, or intended for release there must be cleared with the Pentagon.

But, in addition to the Pentagon's guidelines for policy review, it is not difficult to find indications that each of the services manages to expand on these requirements.

Air Force information officers must submit to the office of information in Washington not only stories that "may receive national coverage" but also those that are "controversial in nature, or which may prove embarrassing to the Air Force or other government agencies."

Air Force information officers are also told that they "are not authorized to submit material directly to nationally circulated magazines, commercial book publishers, or national newspaper magazine supplements." Such material "will be submitted" to the Pentagon.[19]

The Navy's public affairs officers' manual, under the heading of "The Public's Right to Know," advises:

> On occasion, persons not under naval jurisdiction may obtain *unclassified* information which an officer in command believes should not be publicized for reasons of policy or propriety. The officer in command may, when appropriate and with the exercise of utmost discretion, offer such an explanation as may be necessary and *request that the information not be disclosed* further. The Department of the Navy, however, has no authority to enforce such action. [emphasis added]

The manual informs navy public affairs officers that "accounts of the extent of the Navy's disciplinary problems locally and Navy-wide are not releasable, except by the Chief of Information." Moreover, "information on mutinous or seditious acts by naval personnel is not releasable except as approved by the Secretary of the Navy." In contrast: "All items for media release which concern a Navy flag officer or a Marine Corps general will be referred to that officer for his approval."[20]

The manual for army information officers advises that not only interservice controversies but also "intraservice disputes are not proper matters for public discussion."

Indeed, that manual expands on the army's own regulation

that sets forth the clearance requirements for official information. Whereas the latter says that such material is to be reviewed for accuracy and propriety on a "purely advisory basis," the former instructs information officers "not [to] clear material that violates accepted standards of good taste or is otherwise improper. . . ."[21]

The Reviewers in Action

It had taken the young major on the faculty of the economics department at the U.S. Air Force Academy in Colorado nearly 12 months. It had cost him many days on the ski slopes and dozens of frustrating hours in the academy's computer lab. But at last it was ready—an article for a professional but widely read journal. Using cost-benefit analysis and data previously made public, the piece compared the air force's B-1 bomber with the navy's Trident nuclear submarine. Although the footnotes tended to be long and strewn with formulas, he had taken pains to make the article as readable as possible. He was bent on sharing his assessment of the two strategic weapons systems not just with fellow experts; he hoped to reach some of the key Defense policy makers.

His boss at the academy had already told him that the article would have to be cleared by Washington before he could submit it to the journal. Only material destined for the local media could be cleared for release by the academy, the major had found out. He had also been told the piece had to go to the security-review office in the air force's Office of Information, in the Pentagon, part of the office of the secretary of the air force.

In the article, the B-1 did not fare too well. Moreover, the article also accused the navy—ever so politely, but ever so clearly—of playing fast and loose with some figures that made the Trident look considerably better than the facts allowed.

After the third inquiry from the major, the air force security reviewers finally took action—they bucked the article up to the very top of the Pentagon, to the Directorate of Security Review, office of the assistant secretary of defense for public affairs.

Since the article had originated in the air force, it would be automatically routed to the directorate's air force division. And since it involved cost-benefit analysis, it had to be coordinated with Defense Office of Systems Analysis. If the figures in the article disagreed with those of the systems analysis office, the reviewer handling it would have to go back to the author for amendments or clarification.

If the article were only rhetoric concerning the two weapons systems and not serious analysis, then the clearance decision would be made entirely within the security-review directorate, without outside coordination. Had it come from a flag officer with no fewer than three stars, or from a top-ranking civilian defense official, then the reviewer's decision would have to be approved by the deputy director or the director of security review.

Although this is a purely fictional example, the article, if real, would have been given one of three designations. Had it involved no security or policy problems at all, it would have been stamped "cleared for open publication." (That stamp, incidentally, also includes a date and number. A by-product of the "muzzling" tiff between McNamara and Congress, the number tells the director of security review who the analyst was and who reviewed it. It is used to protect the staff's anonymity.) Material in the second category is marked "cleared as amended." Deletions, changes, or additions are necessary before the material will be cleared. If the reviewer specifies that the changes are mandatory, they have to be made before the material is cleared. Material in the third category is completely censored. In such cases a memo is written to the originator spelling out why it was not cleared.[22]

"Overall," said Clay Thompson, head of the air force division in the Directorate of Security Review, "we don't presume to tell them what they can say—only what they can't say." And that, said the retired career air force officer, is particularly important when the Defense Department budget is before the Congress, when overly enthusiastic Defense officials might make statements violating the law, which forbids any outside influence on the members of Congress.

Interservice rivalry, too, is still a problem, Thompson acknowledged. But, he added quickly, it is nothing like "the kind of jungle approach" of the 1950s when the services would battle publicly over budget allocations. Nevertheless, it is still a difficult area for security and policy reviewers. The navy may oppose the air force on the issue of land-based versus sea-based missiles. The navy has a legitimate right to inform the public about its activities, but not by openly belittling a sister service. To judge between the two can be hard.

If such issues are raised in manuscripts destined for the print media, security and policy review decisions are made more carefully than if the same material is to be part of less permanent speeches. And if the material comes from an important Defense official, for instance the chief of staff of one of the services, "it will get tougher scrutiny than if the same thing is authored by a junior officer."

The long-time director of the security review office, Charles W. Hinkle, feels that his directorate's "most difficult job" involves the screening of congressional testimony. As Hinkle described the process, when a transcript comes to the Pentagon from the House or Senate, it goes to the Defense official who gave the testimony. He is allowed to edit it for grammar and syntax but not to change the substance of the testimony. Hinkle's office is "very cautious" about major changes because "we caught hell a few times." Today, he said, changes of substance must take the form of amendments.

From the official, it goes to the office that has authority in the area covered by the testimony. "They take a preliminary security review position" by bracketing in black the parts that should be deleted from the public record. "Where we concur, we put red pencil marks around the black brackets." Hinkle insisted, "Most often our action is restoring what they deleted, mainly because of our exclusive knowledge of what's been released before."

Hinkle stressed that these transcripts of congressional testimony are checked only for security, not for policy. But as a memorandum from Hinkle to his staff makes clear, some material intended for presentation before Congress is also to be reviewed for policy. This memorandum, in use since 1962 to train new review officers, states: "Unclassified prepared statements are reviewed for security and for conflict with established policies or programs. . . . The Director's attention should be invited to any portion which conflicts with established policies or programs and he will, in turn, call it to the attention of the [assistant secretary of defense for public affairs]."[23]

Review for Policy
—and Bad News?

The critical question, of course, is whether the security- and policy-review process results in negative information being withheld or distorted. The question is particularly important because of the close working relationship between the security reviewers and the office through which much Defense information flows to the media—the Directorate of Defense Information. "Standing Operating Procedures" (SOPs)—negotiated and signed in 1968 by the heads of the two directorates—specify how they will cooperate. For its part, security review will keep the information directorate informed of anything it runs across "that is likely to attract national news interest. . . ." On the other hand, the information office "will promptly provide . . . copies of all completed query sheets, releases . . . press conference transcripts and any other releases or guidance on release of information which it appears may not have come to [the reviewers'] attention."[24] Another seven single-spaced, typed pages spell out in detail the procedures to be used.

Although the question of how the review process affects bad news is essential, the answer is evasive. No one in the security-review directorate even keeps track of such mundane information as how many of the items that are submitted are cleared, cleared as amended, or not cleared—much less whether reasons of security or policy mandated changes ordered or clearances denied. The best the director of security and policy review could do was to come up with an estimate: most material is cleared as submitted, very little is not cleared, and the remainder is cleared after it has been amended. The chief of the air force division was only slightly more precise: less than 5 percent— "maybe 2 percent"—is not cleared at all; more than half is cleared as submitted; the rest is cleared as amended.

Given that paucity of information, it is impossible to gauge whether the security reviewers censor material because they fear it would tarnish the Pentagon's image. On the other hand, lack of information does not, of course, prove that they don't manipulate news. Indeed, other bits of information buried in Directorate of Security Review documents raise considerable doubt about the role of the office in the processing of negative, unrestricted information. For instance, the director's job description contains this statement:

> Incumbent is responsible for establishing a program for security review and review for consistency with the policies and objectives of the Department of Defense, the National Government, *and whether the release of the information would be in the best interests of the Department of Defense,* the public and the country as a whole. [emphasis added]

Moreover, the same document implies rather clearly that some information, even if not classified in accordance with prescribed procedures, could be withheld: "Some information, although not classified from a security viewpoint, if released, could give important facts to, or confirm suppositions by, potential unfriendly nations."[25]

This margin of discretion invites several questions. What precisely does the directorate mean by "policy"? Who are its reviewers? What are their qualifications? How are they trained? The latter questions are critical because the reviewers and their bosses wield extensive control. For instance, the job description for the head of the division that reviews all material from the

various components of the office of the secretary of defense
states: ". . . incumbent has full authority to clear or decline to
clear any information proposed for publication and thus affix
the imprimatur of the Department of Defense according to his
personal discretion."[26]

Indeed, the reviewers are encouraged to exercise their own
authority as much as the situation allows: "Whenever possible,
the reviewer should use in-shop resources for solution of problems and resort to coordination outside [the office of the assist-
ant-secretary of defense for public affairs] only where necessary.
Over-coordination slows down the flow of material and imposes
unnecessary burdens on both this Directorate and other
offices."[27]

The usual reviewer assigned to his office, Hinkle said, is a
military officer at the rank of lieutenant colonel or, in the navy's
case, commander. The air force division reviewers tend to have
a research and development background; the army division prefers to include officers from various branches—artillery, infantry, intelligence, and so on; the navy division tends to choose
pilots or others with operational specialities.

Peculiarly enough, the directorate specifies in its selection
criteria for reviewers that officers whose career specialization is
public information are not acceptable. Hinkle came up with
several reasons for this policy. Public affairs officers are shunned
because of "congressional displeasure over PR men"; because
fully qualified public information officers are scarce; and because any well-rounded officer can acquire the skills for the job.
Hinkle did acknowledge, however, that most review officers'
knowledge about public information is "limited." But, he maintained, being part of the public affairs office and using his motto
—"when in doubt, let it go"—counterbalances the reviewer's
lack of public information training.

Preparation for security and policy review begins with a "letter of instruction" that tells the new officer what his duties and
responsibilities are. That, Hinkle said, is followed by on-the-job
training by the division chiefs and includes the use of material
especially compiled for the purpose of indoctrinating new re-

viewers. Sometimes, he said, it takes up to a year "until a guy gets up to speed."

Hinkle was at first unequivocal about what the security-review directorate means by "policy." "The single most important document for policy guidance is the secretary of defense's annual posture statement," he said, adding that the military-posture statement by the chairman of the Joint Chiefs of Staff was the directorate's next most important guide. When pressed as to whether all policy questions were settled on the basis of these documents or whether other sources was used, Hinkle replied: "Our whole library. And it includes everything from statements by the White House press secretary to speeches by the president."

Less glibly, Hinkle eventually said, "Policy isn't codified." He explained that the degree of sensitivity attached to a particular item changes from day to day. Thus, "just because a policy item has been cleared once doesn't mean it's always cleared." For instance, when the secretary of defense changes his position, that change will be reflected in what is cleared. Hinkle quoted former Undersecretary of State George Ball: "You get policy from living in the middle of the stream from day to day."

It emerged, then, that the security and policy reviewers, despite the administrative discretion they can exercise in clearing material for public release, usually are not experts in public affairs matters—although they are part of the Pentagon agency charged with providing the American public with a "maximum of information" about the Defense Department. Indeed, they work in an office whose director's job, in part, officially requires him to use "the best interest of the Department of Defense" as a criterion in the review program, and whose duties are so broad, as his job description indicates, that they may extend to withholding *unclassified* information merely because it "could give important facts to or confirm suppositions by potential unfriendly nations."[28] In the words of a senior official in the Directorate for Defense Information: "We tend to look at a situation in terms of what's releasable, Hinkle in terms of what should be withheld."

And the directorate's fuzzy definition of the concept "policy" suggests that policy review may be used—intentionally or otherwise—to withhold or play down releasable information that is perceived as a potential threat to a particular Pentagon policy. None of these unsettling hints *proves,* of course, that the directorate blue-pencils bad news. But they suggest such censorship may occur.

Some Disturbing Examples

It is not difficult to find instances suggesting censorship. Frank W. Render II, deputy assistant secretary of defense for equal opportunity in 1970–71, recalls that he learned shortly after joining the department to steer away from controversial topics in his speeches and to be "very positive" about the president and the administration in general.

Although none of his speeches ever involved classified material—his work concentrated on race relations in the military—all had to be cleared through the office of the assistant secretary for public affairs. "In those instances when there were things in them that weren't in accord with Defense philosophy, they had to be taken out or changed," he said. He cited a report he wrote after a trip to U.S. military installations in the Pacific to check on race relations.

The report went to his superior, the assistant secretary of defense for manpower and reserve affairs. Then it was sent to public affairs "for more sanitizing." References to specific military bases were deleted. Render insists that the basic tenor of the report was not changed only because someone he knew personally in the office of assistant secretary for public affairs intervened. Nevertheless, a "greatly sanitized" version emerged. "And even then, they didn't seem to like it," Render said, noting that it was quietly released, without the usual press conference.

The department was anxious, he said, to maintain "the image that in the area of race relations the military was the fairest of them all"—which, he added, it once may have been—but not

when he was deputy assistant secretary for equal opportunity.
Gene LaRoque, now director of the Center for Defense Information in Washington, recalls similar experiences. A former rear admiral, he spent 31 years in the Navy, serving as commander of the Sixth Fleet's Fast Carrier Task Force and as a member of the Strategic Plans Staff of the Joint Chiefs of Staff.

As an admiral he frequently had to speak in public. As required by regulations, he submitted his texts for clearance. "Almost every time there was something that needed to be modified —not only for reasons of security. It would come back saying 'contrary to policy.' " Eventually he found it easier to eliminate the material the reviewer found offensive than to change it. He fears that the review process has a chilling effect, keeping new ideas from being publicly discussed. "When you read the speeches by admirals and generals, they are appropriate for the Fourth of July—but they are given on any day of the year. . . . This is no problem when it happens in a small army and when a small budget is involved. But it becomes a rather significant thing when we have a multimillion man military which is now single-voiced."

A. Ernest Fitzgerald was formerly deputy for management systems to the assistant secretary of the air force for financial management. Part of his job was to cut the ever-burgeoning costs of weapons systems wherever possible. In 1966, he and others were trying to get contract managers—inside and outside the Pentagon—to use performance-measurement systems to pinpoint inefficiencies so that "we could avoid perpetuating this waste by building it into subsequent contract estimates." In essence, the object was to get away from using performance on the initial contract of a particular kind of military hardware as the basis for estimating the costs of contracts for subsequent orders of the same hardware.

On one occasion, Fitzgerald made a detailed presentation of this "should-cost" concept before key personnel at the Air Force Systems Command. Most of those attending the meeting asked for copies of his presentation, so Fitzgerald had the tape of the meeting transcribed. When he was preparing to have the transcribed remarks duplicated, he discovered that they had to be sent to the air force's Office for Security Review. That office, in turn, sent Fitzgerald's remarks to the security-review directorate in the office of the assistant secretary for public affairs.

After some delays Fitzgerald was informed that the transcript could not be distributed, not even within the Pentagon. According to Fitzgerald, the director of security review gave these reasons in a letter: "It is a caustic, inappropriate deprecation of the costing techniques which have been sponsored and encouraged by [the office of the secretary of defense] for the past few years."

Fitzgerald's protests that it was his job to improve inefficient management practices got him nowhere. Nor did his argument that security was in no way involved. "Unfavorable comment on established practices might cause the public to lose confidence in the management of the Department of Defense, and this in turn, would undermine security," Fitzgerald was told by security reviewers.

Fitzgerald relates another incident involving a report prepared by a RAND Corporation staff member, Irving N. Fisher, entitled, "Cost Incentives and Contract Outcomes: An Empirical Analysis." Fisher's analysis was also critical of the Pentagon's noncompetitive contracting practices. Fitzgerald recalls that a friend "shipped" him a copy. In the Defense Department, the analysis had been classified "confidential" by "the security review censors." Consequently, Fitzgerald sought to obtain a copy through official channels. He tried the air force's security-review office, where he learned that the classification stemmed not from security considerations but from objections by air force procurement officials. Fitzgerald nevertheless asked that efforts be made to have the Fisher report released. After several months of negotiations involving security-review officials, the report was sprung loose—but only partially, since it still bore the imprint "for official use only."[29]

Fitzgerald himself is a living example of how Pentagon policy considerations affect the way information is handled. In late 1968, he revealed before a congressional committee that the costs for the air force's mammoth C-5A cargo airplane were likely to exceed the original estimates by $2 billion. That revelation cost him his $32,000-a-year job.

Subsequent congressional investigations and other information show that within a year of the 1965 contract award to Lockheed Aircraft Corporation for the development and construction of the C-5A, Defense officials feared substantial cost overruns. The contract, however, had been applauded as "protecting the taxpayers' interests" because it called for the contractor to agree to production costs before he was awarded the production contract. The ostensible aim was to keep him from hiking the price of the actual production models after the contract had been completed. As one student of the C-5A episode said, the Pentagon "lavishly praised itself for having constructed the model of defense procurement." Indeed, according to news reports, then Secretary of Defense Robert S. McNamara called the agreement with Lockheed a "damned good contract."

It was common knowledge inside the Pentagon, however, that the contract had big problems. Almost exactly one year before Fitzgerald appeared before the congressional committee, the Defense comptroller told McNamara that the air force chief of staff had conveyed "incorrect impressions" about the C-5A to the secretary. One of these was that the air force's 1967 estimate for the C-5A contract cost was below that of 1965. Actually, the comptroller wrote, the more recent estimate was almost a half billion dollars higher.

Sure enough, one colonel closely involved admitted to congressional investigators that "C-5A management reports were altered so as to show no overruns." When asked why, the colonel told the House Government Operations Committee: "Because of the nature of the overruns, sir, we felt . . . that the projections we were making were actually estimates, subject to actual proof later on, and that the nature of the estimates was such that if publicly disclosed, they might put Lockheed's position in the common market in jeopardy."[30]

But when Fitzgerald revealed before Congress what Defense knew but wasn't admitting, he lost his job. He was not reinstated until 1973, after the Senate Watergate hearings disclosed that the Nixon White House had been involved in the affair. Fitzgerald's revelations had drawn the ire of a presidential aide, who said in a memorandum that "only a basic nogoodnik would take his official business grievances so far from normal channels."[31]

Concern with the Common Market position of domestic partners of the Defense Department are apparently not the only matters that play a role in whether or not "bad" news is released. Concern for foreign partners seems to play a similar role.

Phil J. Goulding, former assistant secretary of defense for public affairs, tells of a 1966 incident that shows how concern for foreign allies influences decisions on news release. It involved the search off the coast of Spain for four hydrogen bombs scattered when a Strategic Air Command bomber crashed with a tanker while being refueled in midair. According to Goulding, the Defense Department had prepared for such a mishap with a carefully drawn-up public information plan for the "mislaying of thermonuclear weapons." However, the plan was built around the assumption that the bombs would be lost at home: "It did not foresee that we would drop them into someone else's backyard."

As a result, for 80 days Franco's Spain decided what information was or was not released. The Spanish government insisted that nothing official be said publicly about the nuclear weapons aboard the B-52. Only when the chairman of the Spanish Nuclear Energy Board decided to speak out on the subject, more than a month after the crash, could our government acknowledge that three bombs had been recovered but that a fourth was missing. It was finally fished out of the sea by a special navy deep-sea vessel from a depth of 2,850 feet.[32]

Goulding cites other examples to show how foreign policy considerations can keep the Pentagon from revealing to the press—which Goulding feels could show "more maturity and understanding" in its handling of news about government— what it was doing. He points to the use of Thai bases by American fighter-bombers during the Indochina war. Although everyone knew the planes were there, what their destination was, and what they were doing, Goulding says the Thai government insisted, and Defense acquiesced, that the United States not announce the situation.[33]

The Vietnam era is, of course, fertile ground for examples of policy considerations leading to news manipulation. For example, in the fall of 1968, President Johnson announced that the United States would halt the bombing of North Vietnam. Then, in November 1970, during the Nixon presidency, a small task force of specially trained U.S. troops landed about 20 miles outside of Hanoi in an attempt to free American prisoners of war believed to be held at a camp at Son Tay. The dramatic attempt was futile—no U.S. POW's were found in the camp.

Subsequently Secretary of Defense Melvin R. Laird stated at press conferences that there were "diversionary actions" in connection with the Son Tay raid but stressed—in a rambling manner—that "there was no ordinance involved as far as North Vietnam was concerned above the 19th parallel, involved in those diversionary missions which were flown by the United States Navy."

But a few days later, at a White House Thanksgiving dinner for wounded Vietnam veterans, President Nixon told the servicemen: "Of course there were bombing raids going on to distract attention." Indeed, he said, there had been "an air attack on a nearby military base." Some of the servicemen were contacted by a young reporter from the Washington *Post.* When his story appeared on Friday, Assistant Secretary for Public Affairs Daniel Z. Henkin finally admitted that U.S. planes had used "appropriate ordinance" in support of the raid in the area "immediately adjacent" to the camp at Son Tay. He would not specify what he meant by "ordinance," but allowed that "I would not say flatly that no bombs were dropped in the area."

When Secretary Laird met with reporters on the Monday after Thanksgiving, he was asked why he had not mentioned the air raid when he appeared before the Senate Foreign Relations Committee. Said Laird: "I was never asked the question. . . . If you'll read the record, you'll find that the question was not asked. . . . Now I answer questions, but I only answer the questions that are asked."[34]

There are, of course, other examples—including I. F. Stone's incisive "Memo to the AP Editors: How Laird Lied"[35]—but perhaps the most glaring is the Pentagon Papers. The papers show all too clearly what happens to information seen as a threat to a course of action that the Defense Department and the administration have committed themselves to—a threat to support from Congress, various interest groups, and the general public. As Hannah Arendt said in her analysis of the papers: "The crucial point here is not merely that the policy of lying was hardly ever aimed at the enemy . . . but was destined chiefly, if not exclusively, for domestic consumption, for propaganda at home and especially for the purpose of deceiving Congress."[36]

Yet the United States government managed to keep two of the nation's most influential newspapers from publishing some of the Pentagon-compiled documents for 15 days. Thereby, in the words of a historian of American journalism, "the clock was turned back to the time of Henry VIII, who in 1534 imposed licensing upon the English press"[37]—at least until the Supreme Court lifted the restraining orders against the New York *Times* and the Washington *Post*.

Day Thorpe, who served as one of the nine censors in the Office of Censorship during World War II, commented in a 1973 article on the Pentagon papers. Noting the frequent invocation of "national security" in recent years, Thorpe draws a parallel with World War II, "when national security was at least as important as it is today." Thorpe maintains that if a set of documents akin to the Pentagon Papers—"similar in content, similar in classification, similar in shock-value, similar in source"—had been brought into the Office of Censorship during the war, "the newspaper submitting the story prior to its publication undoubtedly would have been told 'There is no objection to the publication of this material.' "

To make his point, Thorpe writes the kind of memo any one of the World War II censors would have been likely to type up for the censorship office's reading file:

1:15 A.M. Brann of the Iconoclast called and said he had a couple of stories could he bring around. I said sure. One was a long document apparently pinched from the War Department files. Pretty hot stuff, a lot of dirt about early complicity with Saigon. No live military plans. Gave Brann our official clearance—"Of no interest to Censorship"—then added my personal unofficial congratulations.[38]

On Policy Considerations:
Officials and Reporters

Officials directly involved in the handling of newsworthy information take different stances concerning the impact of policy considerations on the handling of news. A policy and security analyst in one of the services, formerly a public affairs officer, who asked that his name not be used, saw policy concerns as a factor in the manipulation of unfavorable material. He felt the review process "could be called administrative censorship." He has no qualms about such reviews when they involve statements by senior officials. But in his service, at least, the process exceeds the bounds of legitimacy as far as he is concerned. He found that if an officer writes "an unofficial article on a sensitive topic," he is likely to encounter clearance problems. Not that the article will be flatly rejected. In Kafkaesque fashion, changes will be recommended and amendments required so that the piece will "be in the mill three months or longer. . . . That's why our rejection rate tells you little," he explained. "A good author will see a good article perish because the system takes too long and because people want it to take too long."

But most of the officials said that policy considerations lead to news manipulation only sometimes. The chief of the press division in the office of the assistant secretary for public affairs, navy Capt. Ralph Slawson, said that if the matter were truly significant, leaks would "get it out from under the rug and then it would bite you in the tail." But he agreed that most Defense officials are keenly aware of the political implications of information.

The army's chief of information, Maj. Gen. L. Gordon Hill, Jr., disagreed that news is withheld. "They know they have to get it out," he said, if only because the army prefers releasing bad news—accompanied by an explanation—themselves to someone else's revealing it.

The air force's chief of information, Maj. Gen. Guy E. Hairston, Jr., called lying counterproductive, although "you've got to be careful not to flail yourself." He felt the key is to put bad news in proper perspective. With cost overruns, for example, a release that says " 'Air Force screws Congress' is not what we have in mind." Such issues, he said, have to be explained carefully. "I'm trying to transmit a picture of reality, of truth, keeping in mind that we're all honest." But what happened, then, in the case of the information concerning the C-5A cost overruns? "We must have been out of our mind," replied the general.

The Pentagon correspondents also differed on the question of policy considerations and news manipulation. Joe Kane of *Time* felt strongly that "a Watergate mentality on a reduced level" prevails. Corrdry of the Baltimore *Sun* agreed that policy considerations play a critical role in the way information is handled. To show that this is not a new phenomenon, Corrdry recalled that early in the Korean War, the propeller-driven Mustang fighter was doing well in combat. But the air force chief of staff kept that fact under wraps in fear that his efforts to obtain jet fighters would be undercut.

The *Times*'s John Finney said that policy concerns play only an occasional role. But he was quick to add that the political sensitivity of information most often interferes with information handling at the highest levels of the Pentagon hierarchy.

In short, all the reporters and some officials agree with what a string of examples suggests: Policy considerations can affect the way bad news is handled.

5

In The Name of
National Security

The official position of the United States Department of Defense is that overzealous classification of information is to be avoided; what is needed is a balance between secrecy and publicity.

Or in the words of David O. Cooke, formerly principal deputy assistant secretary of defense for administration, "This government does not and cannot cloak its operations in secret. Information as to our national defense posture and its relationship to allied governments must be given to its citizens."

But, as he further told a congressional committee on the Freedom of Information Act, "on the other hand, consideration must be given to safeguarding that information, the disclosure of which would adversely affect national security and the defense of the United States. The Defense Department is fully cognizant that . . . a balance must be struck between these two necessities."[1]

Those sentiments are not those of the Pentagon alone. Roger C. Crampton, chairman of the U.S. Administrative Conference, told the Subcommittee on Government Information: "It is a difficult job to strike a balance between the right to know, on the one hand, and efficient, effective conduct of government pro-

grams on the other."[2] Crampton's view reflects a pervasive notion which maintains that secrecy is in the public interest because it boosts administrative efficiency.[3] If all that happened
inside a bureaucracy were subject to public scrutiny, this line of
thinking holds, very little productive work would get done.

If secrecy increases a bureaucracy's efficiency, then the Pentagon should be the smoothest-run of federal agencies. The department estimates—that's the best it can do—that more than
a million cubic feet of its active files are jammed full of classified
information. And to classify the material, to safeguard it, to
train personnel for security work, to conduct clearance investigations, and for related matters, the Pentagon spends about
$100 million a year.[4]

That the department must have its secrets can hardly be
disputed. However, this sweeping secrecy permeates the bureaucracy whose job is the management of violence. That orientation to violence results not only in the acceptance of secrecy
in at least some of the Pentagon's affairs, but is also the basis
for many of the professional norms and values that permeate the
department—norms and values that tend to emphasize the adverse aspects of a situation, and to cast events in the least
favorable light.

If that is an accurate assessment, is it possible that what
Pentagon officials perceive to be the efficient attainment of "national security" generates such a climate of furtiveness within
that department that they will tend to withhold—or at least
distort—all but the most "safe" information?

The Length and Breadth
of Pentagon Secrecy

Incidents abound that exemplify the ease with which the
secrecy stamp can be slapped on most anything. Relevant congressional hearings and other material are studded with cases,[5]
including some that would be amusing were their implications
not so serious.

For instance, William G. Florence, a retired air force security specialist who put in 43 years of civilian and military service in government, told the Subcommittee on Government Information of a perplexing case. Some time ago the chief of staff of one of the services wrote a memo to his fellow chiefs stating that too much of the material circulating was stamped "top secret." He proposed cutting back on the classification. Said Florence before the committee: "Believe it or not, Mr. Chairman, that note itself was marked, 'Top Secret.' "[6]

On another occasion, Florence said, someone in the air force decided he wanted to protect—by classifying it—the process used in the production of a special radar-absorbing metal for the F-111 fighter-bomber. According to Florence, there wasn't much that was secret about the material or the way it was produced. A substance of the same type had also been developed in the Netherlands, and comparable radar absorbers had subsequently been patented in Sweden. Moreover, the American developer of the tile-shaped pieces of ferrite had handed out samples as part of a sales campaign. "Despite all of this, the Air Force stamped "Confidential" on both the production process and the tiles themselves," Florence recalled. "To his mind, these were U.S. secrets, and [the involved contractors] were ordered to keep them so."

The story unfortunately doesn't end there. Because of the classification, the manufacturer could not simply discard the metal that was wasted in making the tiles. Over five years, he accumulated 28,500 pounds of scrap metal. Meanwhile, General Dynamics, which installed the tiles in the plane, accumulated 285 barrels of the ferrite scrap. All that waste had to be specially stored and guarded. These measures, says Florence, cost "in the neighbordhood of $400,000."

General Dynamics tried to find a way out of the dilemma. It undertook a study that showed it would cost $600,000 to ship the waste—under guard—to a facility where it could be melted down. But before that was done, security inspectors got into the act, asking the air force in Washington whether the confidential classification was really necessary. That's when Florence be-

came involved. He found out from the director of defense research and engineering that the classification had never been
necessary. "I spent the next 10 months trying to get the classification of the tiles cancelled," he notes. "It was finally dropped
in September 1970, after being in effect for about seven years."[7]

The arbitrariness of the security-classification process is apparently not limited to keeping information secret. It is also
reflected in the way in which information whose unauthorized
disclosure could, for example, "reasonably be expected to cause
exceptionally grave damage to the national security"[8] is suddenly made public. That at least is what Max Frankel, former
Washington bureau chief of the New York *Times,* asserted in
an affidavit filed in connection with the Pentagon Papers case.[9]

As Frankel summed it up, the services conduct classified
weapons research, "only to reveal it for the purpose of enhanc-
ing budgets, appearing superior or inferior to a foreign army,
gaining the vote of a congressman or the favor of a contractor."
In addition, the services use classified information as they compete with one another: "The Navy uses secret information to run
down the weaponry of the Air Force. The Army passes on secret
information to prove its superiority to the Marine Corps."[10] This
practice extends all the way up to the commander-in-chief,
Frankel and others claim.[11] Frankel points to occasions when
presidents made classified material available to him personally
and cites a variety of instances when lesser officials—including
military commanders—did the same.[12]

A task force established by the Pentagon's own Defense Science Board, chaired by a former president of the National Academy of Sciences, wrote in a 1970 report, "The amount of classified scientific and technical information could profitably be
decreased perhaps by as much as 90 per cent by limiting the
amount of information classified and the duration of the classification."

To do otherwise seemed futile to the task force because it is
unlikely that such information will stay classified very long:
". . . it is more likely to assume its knowledge by others in
periods as short as a year through independent discovery, clan-
destine procedures or other means."[13]

Indeed, one of the task force members, Dr. Edward Teller, who played a pivotal role in the development of nuclear weapons and who has a long association with the Defense Department, told the American Physical Society that such overclassification can hurt national security. "There are many who believe that secrecy is needed for reasons of national security," he said in 1973. But, he added, "the fact is that secrecy did not prevent the loss of leadership by the United States in the field of nuclear weapons." In contrast, he said that in the field of electronic computers, where work had been conducted much more openly, the United States "has a position of undisputed leadership." Added Teller: "Secrecy has erected barriers between our country and our allies. The barriers are harmful to science and are a source of weakness to the free world."

As another physicist, who for some years also worked for the Pentagon, told a joint meeting of three Senate subcommittees in commenting on Teller's statement: "Security hides inefficiency."[14]

Some Added Twists

Another little-known aspect of the Pentagon's security-classification system contributes to the pervasiveness of secrecy: "derivative classification."

According to the procedures of the army's office of the chief of information, "Derivative classification devolves upon the person who uses, extracts, reproduces, incorporates, or responds to information which has already been validly classified."[15] What does that mean? In the words assistant secretary of defense Cooke used to explain it to the House subcommittee:

> Derivative classification is involved when any person authorized to receive and disseminate classified information in any form treats that information in the same way as the originator with respect to classification of content and markings. In this case, the derivative classification merely applies the original classification decision already made by the original classifier.[16]

Translating this tortured language, "derivative classification authority" simply means that anyone who incorporates a bit of information already classified into something he's working on can then automatically classify his project secret as well. The Pentagon Papers case once more provides an example. (There are, unfortunately, many others.[17]) The papers were not classified "top secret" by the man who commissioned the study, Defense Secretary Robert S. McNamara, but by Leslie Gelb, head of the task force that wrote and compiled the papers. As Gelb explained it, "since some of the material used in the Papers was top secret, I classified all of them top secret. . . . I just assumed I had the right to originally classify them 'top secret.' I don't know who gave me that right. I remember discussing it with someone . . . I never knew I also had the right to declassify them since I had the right to originally classify them. That comes as news to me. I guess I don't know the classification setup too well."[18]

That Gelb did not know the "classification setup too well" is understandable. Aside from some seminars, symposia, workshops, and other intermittent instructions, Secretary Cooke told the Subcommittee on Government Information, "there is no formal course of training in the security classification of official information which must be completed before officials and employees are permitted to exercise classification authority."[19]

A series of classifications that renders a document more than top secret is even more obscure than the notion of "derivative classification authority." For example the senior official in the office of the assistant secretary of defense for public affairs commented that the assistant secretary and his immediate assistants "carry some pretty exotic clearances." Some were so exotic that he was completely unaware of their existence until he joined the office. The Pentagon insists that use of these special restrictions does not constitute classification above top secret[20]—the highest level authorized by executive order—but that seems to be their effect.

Thus, "NOFORN" means that a classified document is not to be disclosed to foreign governments or nationals. A document marked "SIOP-ESI" means that this is "information at top secret level of such sensitive nature as to require special access and safeguarding procedures."[21] According to former Defense Secretary McNamara, there are about 25 of these special clearances, including some to "which only a handful of people in the government are exposed."[22]

But if there is information classified higher than "top secret," there is also information restricted at a level below "confidential," the lowest category authorized by executive order. Technically, this is not information classified for security reasons; it is restricted for administrative reasons under the label "for official use only."

As a Defense directive makes clear, the only documents that may legitimately be marked "for official use only" are those that can be withheld under exemptions specified by the Freedom of Information Act. But these exemptions tend to be interpreted rather broadly. One of the act categories, for example, stipulates ". . . inter-agency or intraagency memorandums or letters which would not be available by law to a party other than an agency in litigation with the agency" may be withheld. The Defense directive interprets that to include, among other things, "reports prepared on behalf of the Department of Defense by task forces."[23] By that standard, the task force report that found too much classification of scientific and technical information could itself be withheld.

There is, then, a dizzying array of information that is restricted—with astounding ease, at least at times—either by being labeled "for official use only" or by being classified "confidential," "secret," or "top secret" and, in effect, even beyond that through special additional restrictions.

Sanctions for Overzealous Classifiers

Apparently recognizing the ease with which such a system may be abused, various Defense Department rules, regulations, and directives warn all involved not to use national security considerations to withhold releasable information arbitrarily.

For example, the regulation that spells out what material can be considered "for official use only" directs that nothing be withheld because of the possibility that its release "may cause embarrassment by suggesting administrative error or inefficiency." Information officers of all three services are similarly admonished against using the "national security" blanket to cover up bad news:

> Air force: ". . . security should never be used to cloak mistakes."[24]
> Army: "An unfavorable story cannot be withheld on the pretext that it discloses classified or safeguarded information."[25]
> Navy: "No officer in command will resort to unauthorized classification of information or too rigid interpretation of the phrase 'as compatible with security,' in an attempt to avoid controversy or to prevent release of information unfavorable to the Department of the Navy."[26]

But what does the Pentagon *do* to prevent abuse of the classification system? During a hearing of the government information subcommittee, Rep. Ogden Reid asked Cooke, the Pentagon expert on administrative matters, whether any Defense official had so much as been summoned merely to discuss a document's being overclassified. Replied Cooke: "Mr. Reid, I am not aware of any individual who has been brought in in that connection." The committee, not satisfied with that answer, asked Cooke in writing "whether any official or employee of the [Defense] Department has ever been disciplined for such a violation (i.e., classifying information to conceal mistakes, inefficiency, etc.)?" Again, Cooke was not very specific: "In the absence of identification of specific cases, no response can be given to the question. . . ."[27]

Former air force security-classification expert Florence was somewhat more specific before the same committee. To his knowledge, no one had ever been disciplined for overclassifying anything, regardless of the costs incurred for unnecessary security protection, or other damage brought about by keeping the information secret. "But I have seen how rough a person can be treated," Florence added, "for leaving classification markings off of information which he knows to be officially unclassified if someone 'up the line' thinks that a classification should have been applied."[28]

Cooke eventually told the committee that 2,372 administrative penalties were meted out from 1967 to 1971 for failure to protect classified information properly.*When asked: "In how many instances during the same four-year period were changes filed or recommended, administrative hearings held, or penalties of any sort assessed on the basis of overclassification or other excessive restrictions . . . ?" Cooke responded, "Zero instances."[29]

The Pentagon's Track Record
for Releasing Information

To appraise how the department ensures that releasable information is made public, it is once more instructive to refer to March 1972 hearings of the Subcommittee on Government Information, when Robert Beatty, assistant secretary of public affairs in the Department of Health, Education and Welfare, testified on implementation of the Freedom of Information Act. He informed the subcommittee that when a written request for information comes to HEW, the department is very particular about who can deny it. Only 16 persons—the top public affairs officers of HEW's agencies, the main information officer in the department's regional offices around the country, or the director of public services in the office of the assistant HEW secretary for public affairs in Washington—can issue written denials.

---

*Excluding the army, and encompassing only Defense components in the Washington area.

Beatty said, "To make implementation of the act as effective and uniform as possible, HEW's regulations give denial authority to only four individuals for the whole Department here in Washington . . . all public affairs officials."

He noted, "In granting requests for information on records, we normally provide the requested data without charge to the requestor." He furnished the committee with exact statistics of how many written requests for information had been received, how many had been granted, denied, appealed, taken to court. And, he added, he was unhappy about and had been studying the length of time it took for HEW to respond to a request for information—an average of 54 days before action was taken in the case of initial decisions, and an average 71 days on appeals.

Beatty's statements were largely corroborated by the subcommittee's professional staff, usually less than complimentary in assessing how bureaucrats implement the FoI act. "HEW is the only agency in which the public information people appear to be in control of public information," its report said. "When the FoI Act was passed, HEW set up a special office to help administer it." And that special FoI office operates directly under the assistant secretary for public affairs. Moreover, the staff found that "anyone can grant information [in HEW] but only the chiefs of information can deny information . . . And they report they rarely charge fees for search and seldom for copies."[30]

The Difference a Department Makes

In the Pentagon, at least before the amending of the FoI act, the initial decision whether to grant information could be made at any suitable level, by any suitable official so designated. Final denials could be handled by the head of the component—or by someone he designated—with jurisdiction over the record requested. While the assistant secretary for public affairs had a special office with a platoon of reviewers who screen information for breaches of security and compliance with policy, there was no "special FoI office"—not even a single individual—directly under the assistant secretary of defense for public affairs whose job it was to oversee the implementation of the original Freedom of Information Act.

Consequently, it comes as no surprise that when the Pentagon's former general counsel, J. Fred Buzhardt, appeared before the government information subcommittee and was asked how many requests for information made under the FoI Act were denied, he replied: "I guess we really don't know." Nor could he tell the committee the total amount of fees that had been collected in connection with searching for and copying of requested material.[31]

Several important facts about the Pentagon's actions before amendment of the act emerged from interviews with officials in the office of the secretary of defense,[32] the army,[33] the navy,[34] and air force,[35] from Defense Department rules and regulations,[36] and from Pentagon officials testifying before Congress.[37] First, public affairs officers usually played a very minor role, or none at all, in requests made under the act. This was true even in the army, which had an Office for the Freedom of Information which, aside from its main job of screening material for policy, propriety, and accuracy, was to play an advisory role in handling such requests. (That advisory limitation, said one of its review officers, rendered the office "slightly more potent than a eunuch at an orgy.")

Second, most requests were handled by nearly anyone except a public information officer, usually by records management personnel, by various officials in the agencies that generated the documents, and by lawyers, with the attorneys playing a central role in appeals after a request was denied.

Third, security-classification experts were drawn into the process when the information requested was restricted for reasons of national security. Indeed, each of the services has a classification-review committee to determine whether a security restriction is still valid. There is a similar committee at the Department of Defense level, handling requests for material involving classified information held by the office of the secretary of defense, the Joint Chiefs of Staff, and so on. Denials by an individual

service classification-review committee can be appealed to the
Department of Defense committee. As a result of the 1972
revisions of the executive order governing the handling of classified material, there is now also an Interagency Classification
Review Committee, the "court of last resort" for administrative
appeals involving classified information.

Fourth, the handling of a request, particularly if it involved
material the military wanted to restrict, was a time-consuming
process that could take weeks, months if appeals were involved.

Fifth, very few of the requests for information under the
Freedom of Information Act came from the media. Again, no
one could provide exact figures, but the estimates for press
requests ranged from "very few" to "1 percent," to "maybe 5
percent."

FoI Requests by the Media

It is hardly surprising that journalists did not often request
information from a system that took weeks and months to make
a decision. Two well-documented incidents illustrate the problem.

The first involves information classified for reasons of national security only. After President Nixon revised the executive
order governing the classification system, the New York *Times*
requested the downgrading of 51 sets of documents, all at least
10 years old, some going back as far as 25 years. The *Times* did
so because the new order stipulates that classified national security and foreign policy materials 10 years old or older must be
reviewed for declassification on request.

Early in June 1972 the paper asked for the Joint Chiefs'
comments on the Bay of Pigs operation. Six weeks later, the
Defense Department responded that the "papers can be identified and placed under review." But after a fortnight, the Pentagon recanted. "It turns out that the papers in question are in fact
comments on documents prepared as a review separate from the
basic collection of documents which, as you know, is under the

control of the Central Intelligence Agency."

Protesting to the department about its "agile sidestepping and backpeddling," the *Times* on the next day formally requested the papers from the CIA. Receiving no response for nearly a month, the paper renewed its request, stressing its interest in the JCS comments. A reply finally came three weeks later. The CIA said it had no group of documents that had been "formally identified as 'the basic collection.' " The agency also said it had many documents on the Bay of Pigs, and the *Times* request did not meet the executive order's requirements of "sufficient particularity" to allow identification of the papers. Moreover, there were many references among the documents regarding intelligence-gathering methods and sources. Since it was "simply not feasible" to separate the material, the whole file had to be protected; the executive order specifies that material that would reveal intelligence sources and methods did not have to be released, no matter how old.

The CIA further said it had consulted with Defense on the matter, and both agreed that the "JCS documents cannot be released." But the *Times* persisted and appealed to the Interagency Classification Review Committee. By April 1973—10 months after the initial request—the CIA no longer pleaded lack of "sufficient particularity" and said it would review all the material.

That is where the matter stood when Harding F. Bancroft, executive vice-president of the *Times,* recounted the episode before a joint meeting of three Senate subcommittees. He said the newspaper had been successful in five of its requests for classified material 10 years old or older, all but one of which had been addressed to Defense, the CIA, the State Department, and the National Security Council. As he pointed out: ". . . this meager 10 per cent success record has come only after persistent efforts by the *Times,* efforts which are beyond the means of many smaller news organizations, let alone individual scholars and members of the public."[38]

The second incident involves more than material classified for reasons of national security. It is, however, limited to the Pentagon, primarily the army. It dates back to December 1969, when the My Lai incident was prominent in the news. Members of the staff of the *Daily Oklahoman* in Oklahoma City felt that some of the news stories about the massacre contained conflicting reports. As a result, the paper set out to obtain copies of certain records of the army unit involved to help clarify the situation.

Jack H. Taylor, a special assignments and investigative reporter, pursued the matter. In his words, "It took repeated requests over a two and one-half year period before the first records we requested were ever released, and only then after 401 separate items of information were censored—an effort at further suppression that was later overturned on special appeal to the secretary of the Army." But as Taylor stated to three Senate subcommittees jointly examining the problem of government secrecy, those "records raised more questions than they answered and led us to request even more records." All that that produced was "even more intransigence on the part of supposedly responsible officials within the defense establishment."[39]

Taylor and his newspaper requested hundreds of documents and records from the Department of Defense, particularly the army. Of his requests to the army during approximately five years, his records show 159 were denied, 102 granted, 50 partially granted, 133 pending; 41 of his appeals were denied, 8 granted, 2 partially granted, and 42 were pending as of late 1974. Taylor has kept track of the FoI act exemptions cited by the army in the denials. Of the 176 denials, 67 were based on the national security and foreign policy exemption of the act, 41 on the exemption for inter- and intraagency memoranda and letters; the remainder were divided among four other categories for exemption.[40]

Since many of Taylor's requests asked for dozens of items,[41] the army complained to his managing editor about the "unprecedented volume" of requests. The editor didn't take kindly to the pressure. "Aside from the many obvious attempts by the Army to circumvent the law and suppress information to which the public is legitimately entitled," he replied, "there is considerable unnecessary footdragging on the part of supporting Army staff agencies which [the Army] should act to correct."[42]

The complaint stopped neither Taylor nor his newspaper; their requests continued at such a rate that copies of their correspondence with the army, other Defense components, and additional agencies take up more than a foot of space in a filing cabinet drawer of the House Subcommittee on Government Information.

Whether the army was guilty of "covering up" whenever it denied a request from the *Oklahoman* or whether the newspaper was badgering the "green machine" is not the point. The case is instructive because, as with the New York *Times,* it shows how long it takes to obtain information from the Defense Department. According to a tally compiled by Taylor for the chairman of the government information subcommittee in early 1973, three of his requests had been left hanging for more than six months without a definitive response. Eighteen had been pending for 90 days or more, three for 60 days or more, ten for 30 days or more.[43]

Moreover, the volume of correspondence and the incredible detail needed for the identification of each item requested, the further amplification if that identification was not found to be sufficiently particular, the additional mountain of paperwork required if a denied request was appealed, stand as silent witnesses to the time and effort it took to obtain information.

Finally, there is the matter of expense. Eventually the army started to charge the *Oklahoman* for research and copying. Totals are unavailable, but an example is indicative: for biographical information about 54 army officers, the newspaper had to pay $249.40.[44]

In short, not only does the Defense Department restrict an imposing amount of information; but, before the amending of the Freedom of Information Act, it employed a time-consuming, cumbersome system to handle inquiries for information, a system controlled by records managers, lawyers, classification experts, and other "suitable officials."

It will be several years before we know whether the amended act will bring new candor. It is difficult to be optimistic. To be sure, some details will have to change. For instance, the act now specifies precise time limits within which requests and appeals have to be handled. And it is now possible for a judge to review whether a document is legitimately classified; that may cause Defense officials to be somewhat more reticent about hiding behind the national security shield.

However, the Defense Department still does not make it mandatory for public information specialists to be involved in all phases of the process: nor do information specialists ultimately decide if information is released. The head of the agency that has jurisdiction over the record makes the final decision.

The office of the assistant secretary for public affairs has been designated to oversee—although not to control—the Defense Department's freedom-of-information program.

But within the assistant secretary's office, the censors—the security and policy reviewers or, as they are now known, the Directorate for Freedom of Information and Security Review— have been given the job of making the amended FoI act work throughout the Defense Department. Totally forgotten, it seems, is the bitter lesson of the First World War—namely, never to put the censor and the publicity agent under one roof.

Officials and Reporters
on National Security

Pentagon officials and reporters differ sharply on the issue of security classification. What is a classified document to an official may only be a piece of paper stamped "secret" to a reporter. That is not to say that the journalists feel that everything the Defense Department does should be available to them. Kane of *Time* felt that those matters whose release would be "clearly injurious to the U.S. defense" should obviously not be disclosed. But, he and other reporters emphasized, his definition of what would be kept secret is much narrower than the Pentagon's.

In contrast, when asked what information is unreleasable, the officials generally responded without hesitation: anything that is classified. Only a few added that by classified they meant *legiti-*

mately classified; that is, a stamp alone on a document did not automatically mean it could not be released.

Cmdr. Jack M. White, who has spent his entire navy career in public affairs, said "national security considerations were a major factor" in the handling of negative stories. "Someone will always claim the Russians will benefit from it," he said. But most of the public information specialists who saw it as a problem did not see it as a major one. White's colleague, Cmdr. J. W. Busby, director of media productions in the navy's Office of Information, said that news manipulation usually occurs because the individuals involved have spent most of their time working in highly classified fields. "I've seen cases where submariners didn't want anything to go out."

The chief of the air force's Public Information Division saw the situation somewhat differently. The withholding and distortion of information, he said, generally results "from the sincere belief that it is in the best interest of the country."

Nearly as many information specialists rejected the notion that national security considerations play a major role in the manipulation of bad news. William Donohue, who has spent more than three decades in information-related work and who now heads the army's Office for the Freedom of Information, snapped, "The whole notion of a climate of secrecy is sheer garbage."

Most of the public information specialists who felt that national security considerations did play a role in the handling of negative news were career naval public affairs officers. The navy has officially acknowledged that overzealous classification hinders the flow of information. Unlike its two sister services, it recently took a long, hard look at its public affairs operations, generating a penetrating, little-known study. One of the bottlenecks the 200-page report found in the navy's news dissemination efforts in Washington was the "tendency to overclassify [which] still exists, though not as much as it once did."[45]

Most of the journalists felt national security plays a major role in the way bad news is handled. The AP's Fred Hoffman was most succinct: "They use it to cover their ass." Charles Corrdry said, "They've been in a state of crisis almost all of the time since

World War II. . . . They overclassify and they admit it." Joe Kane argued that the overuse of the secrecy stamp is inevitable. "It's a reflection of the element of surprise. You don't tell your enemy what you're doing, and that carries over to not telling your opponent what you're doing." Some members of the Congress and the media, he feared, are seen as such opponents.

Steinhauser of the *Armed Forces Journal* expanded on that theme. "What they do is to say they can't give you something because it may aid the enemy, but it actually has nothing to do with the enemy. Particularly when it comes to spending money, they'll put the national security blanket on it." He cited an interview with an officer in charge of a tank project plagued by cost overruns. The officer insisted that the material Steinhauser sought was classified, when "in fact, it was already contained in published congressional testimony."

A chilling indication of the lengths to which the Pentagon will go in the name of national security emerged from the journalists' remarks.

Back in 1963, Hanson Baldwin, then the military editor of the New York *Times,* reported that the FBI was being used to track down the sources of leaks in various federal agencies, including the Defense Department.[46] Two years later, in 1965, a Washington correspondent reported that the office of the secretary of defense had established an investigative arm to track down the sources of news stories, in at least one case "investigating and interrogating the reporter himself."[47]

In 1966 the Defense writer of the Washington *Star* reported that in one such investigation 120 persons, "by count of the Defense Department, were asked if they would take a lie detector test. The whole thing blew up in public and the Department officials didn't go through with it. . . ."[48]

In 1969 the office of the assistant secretary for public affairs was quoted as acknowledging that an investigation had been made to find the sources of news stories written by Washington journalist Sarah McClendon.[49] And in 1971, reported David Wise, Pentagon correspondents were troubled to find out the press room had been searched overnight by the "Pentagon

Counterintelligence Force." The agents left cards on some reporters' desks that said: "An inspection of this office by the
Pentagon Counterintelligence Force revealed no violations of
security regulations."[50]

Several of the regulars interviewed for this study said such
investigations had continued into the 1970s. Hoffman of the AP
recalled that during the 1973 Middle East War he gained access
to intelligence information indicating how successful the Israeli
air force had been during the fighting. "They had five simulta-
neous investigations to find out where I got that information."
Bob Schieffer of CBS. News said that after he reported on a
major buildup during the Vietnam War, investigations were
conducted to determine where he obtained his information.
"Yes, it happens all the time," said *The Washington Post*'s
correspondent, adding that he feels it is done not just to find the
sources but to intimidate other potential sources within the
department. Corrdry, too, said, "I know they send these guys."

6

On Selling
and Vested Interests

Just as the secretary of defense sets forth the department's "public information principles," so, too, the army, navy, and air force all routinely declare that the aim of their PR programs is to inform the American people.

The army tells its information officers that the "American public has a right to maximum information concerning the Army and its activities. . . . Nothing must inhibit the flow of unclassified information to the American public."[1] The air force proclaims that its public information mission "is based on the policy that the full record of the Air Force is available to the American people. . . .";[2] the navy points out to its public affairs officers that the "right of the public to be fully informed" is one of the Defense Department's basic principles.[3]

Indeed, recent secretaries of defense, in their widely circulated, publicly posted set of information principles, have all parroted the admonition, "Propaganda has no place in the Department of Defense public information programs."

But the much less visible *Dictionary of Military and Associated Terms,* published by the Joint Chiefs of Staff, defines public information somewhat differently. It calls it "information of a military nature, the dissemination of which through news media is not inconsistent with security, *and the release of which is considered desirable or nonobjectionable* to the responsible releasing agency"[4] [emphasis added].

That definition and the department's record of engaging in a wide range of self-serving PR activities suggest that Pentagon officials may see their job of informing the public in terms of "selling" their department. Indeed, the Joint Chiefs of Staff definition of public information is clearly reflected in key directives that prescribe the scope of each service's PR program.

The army says that the aim of its public information program is to "gain public understanding and support of the Army's role in a sound national military program" and to "inspire public confidence in the Army's ability to accomplish its mission now and in the future."[5]

The air force asserts that its program aims to help the American public understand the "aggressive threats to the United States and the Free World, the dangers inherent in complacency, and the national policy on the best military structure to deter, limit or win war." Moreover, it wants Americans to comprehend the "need for constant, controlled modernization and improvement of Air Force equipment to keep ahead of any potential aggressor. . . ."[6]

The navy's public affairs directives contain similar statements,[7] but a recent in-house study by a high-level task force of its public affairs program is much blunter. Overall, the study is concerned with injecting more professionalism into the program. However, in a discussion of how to handle PR problems raised by modern weapons system, the report suggests, "Public affairs program must take the initiative with the press, the public and the Congress . . . friends . . . and foes . . . must be identified in an early stage. . . . All aspects of a system, whether positive or negative, must be identified. Skilled public affairs officers, in sufficient numbers, will anticipate public affairs problems and accentuate the positive."[8]

The little-known Defense Information School at Fort Benjamin Harrison, Indiana, uses a handbook that indicates how important "selling" is in Defense PR.* The handbook "as closely as possible conforms to military public affairs doctrine and policies published by the Department of Defense and the individual Armed Services." The first chapter introduces the student to "military public affairs." He learns that "favorable public opinion is considered the key-stone of the successful accomplishment of the Department of Defense mission."

In a chapter tracing the history of public relations, the student discovers that the "end result of public relations is favorable public opinion toward and public acceptance of an individual, idea, product, service or institution." To make sure the point is not missed, the chapter summary announces: "Public relations is practiced to favorably influence public opinion and human behavior."

The introduction to the following chapter states: "Reduced to its simplest terms, public relations is an effort to influence public opinion and thereby elicit a specific favorable reaction from certain specific publics as an organization." And again in the summary of that chapter: "The objectives of public relations are to conserve or keep favorable opinion, crystallize unformed or latent opinion and change hostile opinion."

Not until the seventh chapter, on "public information," does the tenor of the handbook change. Now the student is told that the information officer "must use the principle of 'maximum disclosure with minimum delay.'" That theme is expanded in

---

*Established after World War II, this school started out as the Army Information School at Carlisle Barracks, Pennsylvania. As military public relations grew, so did the school. Over the years, it changed its name and location, finally ending up in Indiana in 1965 with the information training programs of the various services brought together under its umbrella. Lately its budget has been close to $1 million and its faculty, half of which is civilian, has stood at about 85. Of nearly 1,500 students there in one recent year, roughly four-fifths were active-duty enlisted personnel, the remainder officers.[9] Although it is hardly known outside the Defense Department, the school is important because its public information officer course "is the only training that many individuals receive before being assigned to information jobs."[10]

a chapter dealing with the handling of adverse public affairs situations. It cautions, for instance, that "bad news cannot be suppressed. Attempts to hide bad news make the military look dishonest."[11]

Despite the eventual admonition that information officers are to adhere to the principle of "maximum disclosure with minimum delay," the heavy emphasis on the "selling" aspect of Defense Department PR in the school's handbook and in its other activities apparently leaves its mark.

An officer who later became the head of the school's Public Affairs Division made a study to test the "validity of the school claim that 'maximum disclosure with minimum delay' best portrays the mood of overall instruction" at the institution. He asked 156 army information officers which of three statements "best describes the philosophy of the school's approach to news handling:" (1) "Strict adherence to the principles of 'maximum disclosure with minimum delay' and straight, unbiased news coverage of all military events"; (2) "maximum disclosure with minimum delay, combined with a light public relations touch"; and (3) "public relations releases designed to cast favorable light on the military."

A light public relations touch in the school's programs was chosen by 39 percent. Another 13 percent thought "whitewash" was the more appropriate description. And 48 percent agreed that "maximum disclosure with minimum delay" marked the school's philosophy. Interestingly, the higher the rank and the greater the experience of these officers, the more they questioned that the school preached maximum disclosure with minimum delay.

Putting it another way, more than half of the surveyed information specialists felt that the Defense Department's information school, rather than fostering strict adherence to the sententious maximum-disclosure, minimum-delay notion, does in fact advocate the selling approach.[12]

Reporters and Officials
on Selling the Pentagon

This orientation of the Defense Information School is part of the evolution that has led to the Pentagon's "new public relations." It is a facet of the work environment of the journalists and information specialists who were asked whether bad news is concealed or distorted because it interferes with the Defense Department's image-building efforts.

As a group, the officials were evenly divided. Nearly half felt that the preoccupation with positive PR plays a role in the handling of unfavorable information. Most of the others maintained it no longer does.

A senior army information officer agreed that news is manipulated at times, but not because of an overemphasis on self-serving PR. But then, at another point, he pulled a 12-page document from his desk which, as far as he was concerned, still sums up appropriately what the army's public information program is all about. That document's first page proclaims that "this memo was used in modified form in 1947 . . . to brief Gen. Dwight Eisenhower, to sell him on the peacetime PR function." Such a public relations program is essential, the memo holds, if the army is to have the public support it needs. And the model for such a program is the American corporation, where "people are thinking in terms of public attitude as they evolve their plan. Their plan is a product—maybe it's a sausage grinder—or a bath tub—it's all the same. If they can't make the public understand it needs this sausage grinder, they are wasting their time and effort."

Army public relations should be "the counterpart of the corporation's combined public relations, sales promotion and advertising agencies." In setting forth the details of a PR program for the post-World War II army, the memo makes some interesting points. The wartime military security-review function might be "a very profitable arrangement for us since we can correct false ideas and assumptions and, in some cases, we can change a writer's viewpoint from taking a mean crack at us to giving the devil his due." After repeatedly inveighing against the hiding of embarrassing stories, the memo concludes that the goal is "to develop our program so that we can lay down mass PR fire when and as we need it."[13]

The "professional Army" knows the country's security requirements, but the public too must be convinced.

Other information specialists were as inconsistent as this memo. Most agreed that information officers will not release bad news as quickly as good news. But not all felt overemphasis on self-serving PR was the reason.

Navy Cmdr. Jack M. White insisted that the problem lies with ignorant commanding officers or public affairs officers, not with self-serving PR.

Col. Robert Hermann, chief of the air force's public information division, saw the problem in a similar light. The information specialist, he pointed out, is on the commander's management team. "He should look at matters from the public communicator's perspective to help the commander get his job done. His job is to advise the commander." But what if the commanding officer does not accept the information officer's advice to release unfavorable news? "The IO doesn't have many alternatives. If the CO doesn't take his advice, that's all he can do."

With that, Hermann and White had touched on two factors not previously mentioned in connection with the concealing and distortion of negative, newsworthy material. And these two factors—the furtive commanding officer and the incompetent information specialist—were to crop up again and again.

The officials, however, were not alone in their ambivalence over the question of whether zealotry in the pursuit of a shiny image is a likely cause for the manipulation of unfavorable information.

The correspondents were similarly divided—half saw the general emphasis on "selling" as a factor in news manipulation; the others didn't. But like the officials, they agreed that information officers put out bad news less quickly. "The military PR book says to get it out and over with," said Hoffman of the AP. "In fact, the opposite happens. They obfuscate, delay, and all it does is fester." Bob Schieffer of CBS said that at the Pentagon, the "uglier the story, the harder it is to get information," mainly because of "too much training in corporate PR," engendering attitudes that are misplaced in a public agency.

But the blame was not heaped soley on the information officer. Finney of the *Times* pointed out that most of the competent public information specialists put out bad news quickly, although usually they try to put a good face on it. But even then, he said, some commanders do not go along with these competent information officers. Richard Levine of the *Wall Street Journal* agreed that most good public affairs officers understand the problems of the media, "but they are still officers and have to take orders."

Indeed, half of the correspondents seconded the notion that certain commanding officers doom information release.

The Vested Interests of the Information Officer

Some writers suggest that news is withheld because of the information officer's vested interest. It is asserted that the *raison d'être* of any government public relations office is to advance the interest of the agency it serves. Therefore, the argument holds, the PR specialist will seek to confine what he releases to material that will bring credit to his superiors.[14]

Most of the journalists rejected this hypothesis. But many agreed that a variety of pressures exerted on the information officer from above do affect news dissemination because they tend to severely restrict his role in the expediting of information, sometimes to the point of neutralizing it.

UPI's Warren Nelson, for example, said that some career information officers in the services have complained to him about what happens to "blackeye" stories when they are released through the office of the assistant secretary for public affairs. "A lot of nuances are removed and confessions of guilt deleted," he has been told. "These IOs don't like this massaging one bit." However as Steinhauser of the *Armed Forces Journal,* himself a retired colonel, sees it, the problem does not lie with the information officer: "The CO decides what's released."

The increasingly familiar refrain about the commanding officer was picked up by the information specialists as well. Some, like Capt. Ralph L. Slawson, chief of the press division in the office of the assistant secretary for public affairs, even agreed the information officer's vested interest in making his unit look good is a factor. However, Slawson said usually the type of public affairs officer not intelligent enough to understand that "he is not primarily responsible to his commander, but to the American public" falls into this category.

A senior navy public affairs officer expanded on that theme. "Where the DuPont PR man would be expected to keep quiet or put the best face on [the unfavorable news], I don't view our work that way. Our role is to get the whole story out." But, "as a working thing, the corporate thing is true; that is, to play it down or keep it quiet." Furthermore, every naval public affairs officer is responsible to his commander: "You have to convince the CO. If he says 'no,' it's 'aye, aye, sir.' "

The army's chief of information did not see the vested interests of public affairs officers as a factor in the manipulation of unfavorable news. The chief of his public information division, Col. Rolf Utegaard, was defensive on the issue. "We're not flacks," he said. "We think we're doing a good job."

Thus most of the reporters and officials agreed that the information specialist may manipulate news either because they do not realize that their responsibilities differ from those of corporate public relations experts or because they must comply with the orders of superiors—and not just because of their vested interests.

Restraints on the Military
Public Information Specialist

A multitude of restrictions besides those already mentioned affect the handling of information by public affairs officers.

The interview is, of course, one of the main information channels between the Pentagon and the media. Although the 1960s requirement that interviews be monitored has been rescinded, the handling of interviews, press conferences, and briefings is still scrutinized. For instance, a section of the regulation on general army information policies stipulates that at the Department of the Army level, "normally, interviews and press conferences will be arranged by the Office, Chief of Information and, where appropriate, attended by an information officer or by a technical liaison officer of the Army agency concerned."[15] The SOPs of that office are somewhat more specific. They direct that the public information division "arranges, monitors and reports interviews by news media and magazine and book representatives with Army personnel, both military and civilian."[16]

Navy public affairs regulations are less emphatic, stating, "A public affairs officer should be present only if desired by the person being interviewed."[17] The navy's Office of Information stipulates that when a request comes for an interview with an admiral, it is approved by the public information division: then the interviewee is asked "if he desires an advisor." In the case of interviews involving certain sensitive subjects—for instance, the F-14 plane—the request must be coordinated with the vice-chief of naval operations. Before the interview, according to navy procedures, the public affairs officer is to discuss with the official to be interviewed who the interviewer is, what the "ground rules" for the interview will be, which areas "are sensitive from a public affairs aspect," and so on. At the beginning of the interview, the information officer is to "cover the ground rules and what they involve," and during the interview he is to "take notes on what is said."[18]

No such suggestions were found in relevant air force public information regulations and manuals. But these publications do deal with media access to air force installations. Information officers in the field are told they "may authorize local representatives of bona fide information media or reputable freelance writers to visit installations under Air Force jurisdiction."[19] Such access can be critical, since officials can control information more easily if reporters can't get to a place or a person. Air force information officers are warned that when a story may be controversial, might receive national coverage or "prove embarrassing to the Air Force," the media access request has to be coordinated with the air force information officer in the Pentagon.[20]

The army is less specific, but also stipulates that its installations are open to journalists in connection with "a matter of local interest" or spot news. All other requests have to be approved from Washington.[21] The navy public affairs officer is also given guidelines for the "embarkation of media representatives," but no mention is made of Pentagon approval being needed.[22]

The Pentagon correspondents had encountered problems of access. Two find that some officials instruct secretaries not to put through telephone calls from the press but to refer them automatically to a public affairs officer. As a result, when they now call certain offices, they no longer identify themselves as reporters. The office for International Security Affairs was singled out as a case in point. Said one newsman: "If you call a secretary there, you get a stone-wall attitude."

Levine of the *Wall Street Journal* pointed out another dimension of the problem of access to military installations. When he went to Panama to do a story on how the United States guards the canal, he said, "I was escorted everywhere." Such escorts, he added, slow him down. Steinhauser of the *Armed Forces Journal* mentioned similar problems when visiting military installations. "They won't let you roam. . . . They don't insist on an escort, but one is always present. They are there 'to give you the full story,' but they really don't, of course."

Another tactic limiting the flow of information is "chopping" —the in-house coordination of the blue tops and the answers provided to queries from reporters. Chopping works similarly in the military services and in the office of the assistant secretary of defense for public affairs. The chief of the assistant secretary's press division said that under normal circumstances, when a given matter comes to his attention, an action officer is assigned. He or she contacts the agency dealing with the subject—manpower or the comptroller, for example. Their replies come back to the press division, a process that can take days. If the answers come from one of the military services, their accuracy is checked with knowledgeable officials in the office of the secretary of defense.

Once the answer is complete, it may be checked with the security-review directorate for security, policy, and propriety considerations. If it involves a routine policy issue, it usually will also go to the director for defense information or perhaps the assistant secretary for public affairs. If it involves a sensitive policy issue—such as military aid to Middle East countries or arms reduction talks with the Soviets—it may go to the deputy secretary of defense or the secretary himself. Indeed, it may have to be coordinated with other government agencies, for instance, the State Department or the White House.

An actual case provides an apt illustration of chopping. The navy's information office in the Pentagon received a call from a California newspaper querying various aspects of Iran's purchase of a fighter aircraft and the training of Iranian pilots at a California naval facility. Although the answer was due late the next day, the chopping in this case delayed it for four days. It involved, among others, the Defense Security Assistance Agency, the office of the vice-chief of naval operations, and the comptroller's office. When the process was completed, the navy was directed to refer the reporter to the Iranian government for information on the training of the pilots.

Clearly, there is a need for the coordination of information before it is publicly released, given the size of the Defense Department, the complexity of the issues it deals with, and the possible domestic and foreign ramifications of its words and deeds. As Defense officials like to say, "The executive branch must speak with one voice." But the process also sets up a series of filters through which information is strained, at times very slowly.

In the office of the assistant secretary for public affairs, the head of the press division estimated that queries are usually handled within one day, and action taken on most within a week. In the air force information office no one knew the average length of time needed to reply to queries. The army public information division said that depending on the urgency and content of the request, the reply can take from an hour or two to "much longer," particularly when it involves legal matters or requires coordination with the Congress.

When the navy decided to reassess its public affairs operations, it found that "the number of 'chops' on any one query varies according to the subject matter and how 'hot' it may be —sometimes, from sources to completion, there may be as many as 10 to 15 chops. All of these steps add to a time-consuming process."[23] As a result, according to Cmdr. Jack B. Finkelstein, the director of the public information division in the navy's Office of Information, steps were taken to reduce the time taken to answer queries. By mid-1974, said Finkelstein, it took one day to accomplish what had required four days 1½ years earlier. But Finkelstein acknowledged that "sometimes chopping still dilutes information to the point where it is nonresponsive." At that point, he hoped, his office steps in and tries to reverse the dilution process.

The reporters saw chopping in the same light but emphasized the delays and nonresponsiveness they have encountered. As Steinhauser put it, "You ask a question and they give you exactly what you asked for—when three more words would have really completed the picture." The AP's Hoffman has seen chopping "take weeks, depending on how edgy the people are up the line." He finds that the result is an "elephantine process," in the end self-defeating because the late or vague reply is useless to the journalist.

Information officers are further restricted by a Defense Department policy that assistance on audio-visual projects will be provided only if it benefits the Pentagon or is in the "national interest."

One example is instructive. The weekly activity report the Directorate of Defense Information sent to the assistant secretary for public affairs on December 7, 1973, includes this entry: "Informed Bridgett Potter, Pallomar Pictures, that the Army has determined 'no conceivable advantage could accrue' from a film based on the story of Lt. Pelosi as a cadet at West Point; therefore, assistance in filming at the academy not approved."[24]

What makes this entry noteworthy is that James Pelosi, upon graduating from the U.S. Military Academy, disclosed that he had been subjected to the West Point "silence." He had been found guilty of cheating by a cadet honor board. However, on appeal to the academy superintendent, the cadet honor committee's decision was not upheld, so that Pelosi could not be legally expelled from West Point.

The corps of cadets, in response, reverted to its traditional practice of "silencing" any cadet found guilty by the honor committee who could not be forced to leave. Pelosi was ostracized and harassed; he was isolated in a room of his own and banished to a special table in the cadet dining hall. He endured the extralegal treatment for more than a year and a half and eventually graduated.

At that point, his story appeared on page one of the New York *Times*. The reaction to the disclosure of the "silence" was such that a few months later another story appeared on the front page of the *Times*, its headline stating, "Cadet Committee at West Point Does Away With 'The Silence.' "[25]

Against this background the army decided—and the office of the assistant secretary for public affairs concurred—that "no conceivable advantage could accrue" from a film based on Pelosi's experiences. That decision was based on a Pentagon directive delineating "audio-visual public affairs responsibilities and practices." Audio-visual material encompasses everything from still photography, motion pictures, television films, videotapes, radio tapes, and motion picture stock footage to "associated materials and activities." It specifies that the "production, program, project or assistance *will benefit the* [department] or otherwise be in the national interest. . . ." It also advises that the assistant secretary for public affairs is responsible for "approval for public release of [Defense-] generated audio-visual material" unless it is of local interest only or "deals with spot news events which take place without prior planning or knowledge. . . ."[26]

Another directive specifies that in the production of nongovernment motion pictures and television programs, the Pentagon will make commitments for assistance "only . . . after approval of script and list of requirements" and if the project is determined to be of benefit to the department or "otherwise in the national interest."[27] This second directive goes so far as to specify that the department will only provide stock footage if it approves of the way it will be used.

Norman T. Hatch, chief of the features division in the Directorate of Defense Information, explained the rationale behind this policy: neither the office of the secretary of defense nor the military services "see any need to help beat themselves over the head with a bad film." He denied the policy was a form of censorship: "We're not denying any information." It may be more difficult for a producer to make his film or television program without Pentagon assistance, but it can be done, Hatch insisted.

One mass communication researcher who studied the effect of Pentagon influence on war movies made during 1948–70 found, however, that the department's audio-visual assistance policies have had significant effect. "The military did influence its own portrayal by the American film industry. The result was not a complete perversion of how the movies would have portrayed the military without assistance. However, the intrusion . . . does provide an example of what can happen when a mass medium relinquishes editorial control in return for economic favors."[28]

Army, navy, and air force regulations and manuals all reflect adherence to the same general policy. In addition, each service has a variety of other rules governing the release of audio-visual material its produces or helps to produce.

Thus, army information officers are told: "Every consideration will be given to photographing women in uniform other than the field (fatigue) or training duty uniform and in jobs that are not associated with weapons or field training." If a civilian journalist is on an army post for the "purpose of photographing women in field or training uniforms, with weapons, or participating in field or bivouac training, *an information officer will accompany that reporter and assist in obtaining photographs that are in keeping with a favorable image of Army women*" (emphasis added).

The same regulation spells out which type of army photographs taken in hostile areas is releasable and which is not. Unreleasable are pictures of dead or wounded not identified by name and of casualties whose next-of-kin have not been notified. But there is also a rather broad ban on releasing pictures "showing killed and/or wounded personnel in large numbers." Indeed, official army photographs "of combat dead under field conditions normally will not be released to public media," the pre-My Lai regulation specifies.[29]

There are other rules and guidelines for the military information officer, prescribing his role and affecting the flow of information from the Defense Department to the public through the media. Indeed, he is even given guidance on the use of informal information channels—background press briefings, "deep backgrounders," off-the-record conditions, and much more.[30] This collection of directives seems to support the journalists and officials who say that the pressures and restrictions imposed on the information officer from above cause the manipulation of bad news, not his supposed vested interests as a public relations man.

Or to put it another way, neither the selling of the Pentagon nor the vested interests of the information specialists can be wholly blamed for news manipulation. But other factors did move onto center stage unexpectedly: restrictions imposed from above, the incompetent public information officer, and the commander who thinks his outfit's business is no one's but his.

7

"The Public's Right
to Know Is Not
the Controlling Factor"

America's career military officers tend to adhere to an ideology peculiar to the profession of arms.[1] This ideology, which has deep historical roots[2] and has been labeled the "military mind" or "military ethic," has been probed by serious students of the military ranging from C. Wright Mills to Samuel P. Huntington.[3]

Huntington, who has dealt with the concept more extensively than most, maintains that the origins of the military ethic are deeply embedded in a conservative, Hobbesian view of man that "holds that man is evil, weak and irrational. . . ." Or as he puts it at another point: "As between the good and the evil in man, the military emphasizes the evil."[4]

If these are the values held by the military—a uniformed hierarchy whose perch can be reached only after a long struggle up many lower rungs, and only after being carefully socialized —how will they affect news handling? Will information be withheld or distorted if those primarily involved in handling it are members of this career-oriented, closed military bureaucracy?

Reporters and officials refuted this view. Only one singled out the career military man as bearing responsibility when blackeye stories are manipulated. No other evidence contradicts that assessment. While the career officer was thus exonerated, several officials once again blamed the commanding officer or the incompetent information officer.

As far as Lt. Col. C. B. Kelly, head of the Operations Forces Branch in the air force Office of Information, was concerned, the problem lies mainly with those who rise to command without understanding "the information business" and the need "for full and complete disclosure"—a principle based less by altruism than pragmatism: "It's not that we're so goddamn honest—it's that we're so goddamn practical." To await the invariable leak instead of releasing the story is to allow a manageable PR problem blossom into a public information fiasco.

Reinhold Herman of the army's Office for the Freedom of Information thinks information manipulation can be traced to information officers concerned about the rating their commanding officer will give them, which can be of critical importance to their entire career. "It is a closed society, and [information officers] must protect their rater. Loyalty, therefore, is to the command, not the public. That's the nature of the beast."

If it is not the career officer high atop the Defense hierarchy who hinders the flow of bad news, is the fearful subordinate on a low rung of the Defense bureaucracy responsible? Does he, to protect himself, keep such information from being passed upward?[5] The reporters and officials said that subordinates' fears may at times result in the withholding or playing down of unfavorable information. But they also stressed the sheer size of the Defense Department, the complexity of the issues involved, the chopping requirements, the great distances between the Pentagon and some of its components where incidents occur, all affect the handling of adverse information. The department, however, has a variety of mechanisms that help overcome these problems and ensure that the information will reach those officials authorized to release it.[6] "If a guy holds back, he's courting disaster," said Capt. Fred Ellis, senior public affairs officer of the Navy Materiel Command.

Most journalists also felt that if the issue is important enough, the information will be forwarded by subordinates, fearful or otherwise. Steinhauser, who had himself spent 28 years in the army, "never knew of important information that the guy on the top didn't know—even if he didn't want to know it." In the military, he said, "the cardinal sin is to have a boss who is surprised."

A variety of incidents—the C-5A cost overruns, the My Lai massacre, General Lavelle and the unauthorized bombing raids, the Gulf of Tonkin case—generally exonerate the subordinate. Even Phil Goulding could cite only one prominent incident that occurred while he was assistant secretary of defense for public affairs in which his office misinformed the public because fearful subordinates—in this case, an air force colonel in Southeast Asia—had deliberately distorted information about the strafing by U.S. planes of a Soviet freighter at anchor in a North Vietnamese port. Goulding did have problems extracting accurate information quickly during times of trouble. But he had ways of dealing with the problem, including a highly effective one: Whenever a major incident erupted, he immediately dispatched one of his experienced public affairs officials to the scene.[7]

The Responsibility to Keep the Public Fully Informed

Thus, neither the career military man nor the fearful underling turned out to be very promising leads in the search for clues to explain why the Pentagon processes bad news as it does.

Not so with the penultimate factor explored in this book. How badly unfavorable news is distorted seems to vary in accordance with how clearly the officials who handle it understand their responsibilities as public servants. If, for instance, they are not aware that the Freedom of Information Act limits what the federal government can legitimately withhold, then bad news is likely to be manipulated.

To plumb that awareness, I interviewed journalists and information specialists, examined the career patterns and professional status of information officers, searched for training programs on the subject of information release, particularly at the Defense Information School, and looked at how one of the services is trying to get its senior officers to rethink their role in military-media relationship.

Most of the officials regularly involved in the handling of newsworthy information feel that the lack of a sense of responsibility to keep the public fully informed is a factor in the manipulation of negative stories. Lou Arrants, chief review officer in the army's Office for the Freedom of Information (the office responsible for counseling personnel on questions related to the Freedom of Information Act and providing instructions at various key conferences on the subject)[8] agreed that the official who does not realize his responsibility toward the public is a problem. But he blamed the commander. "We really don't teach the right people—the commanders," he said. Those views were echoed by Arrants's colleagues, and even the director of his office acknowledged that army personnel may not always be fully aware of their legal obligations.

The air force chief of information, Maj. Gen. Guy E. Hairston, Jr., also felt that "some people in the air force don't realize their responsibilities to the public." He acknowledged that he himself did not know the provisions of the Freedom of Information Act. "But I have guys around here who do—at least I hope we do."*

Most of the reporters, too, thought that the lack of a sense of public responsibility by Defense officials led to news manipulation.

Levine of the *Wall Street Journal* described the military's attitude toward the press as "we've-got-this-problem-and-what-are-you-going-to-do-about-helping-solve-it." They do not un-

---

*Of the officials interviewed, all of whom are either career public affairs officers or in high-level public affairs jobs throughout the Pentagon, less than half were clearly knowledgeable about what can and cannot be released.

derstand that "I'm not a member of their team. They don't understand the adversary relationship that does and should exist."

Corrdy of the Baltimore *Sun* felt the lack of a sense of responsibility to keep the public fully informed was only an occasional factor. "I'm not sure that the responsibility occurs to these people to tell you what they are doing." Below the level of the appointed Defense official, he said, there is a bureaucracy that feels the government belongs to it.

The Training and Careers of the Military Information Specialist

Those officials who agreed that the lack of a genuine sense of responsibility to keep the public informed was a pervasive problem had a specific suggestion: to discover why, take a look at the career patterns and status of military public information specialists, and examine the training and education they receive.

In the navy, public information is recognized as a permanent career field for officers. Although some enter the field directly after being commissioned, an officer usually becomes a public affairs specialist only after serving four to eight years in various other jobs, normally including a tour of duty at sea. With such experience behind him, he is eligible for a career in public information work. Part of that career includes training on the job, attendance at the Defense Information School or other short courses and, when possible, work on a master's degree related to communications.[9]

The air force's approach is similar, although public information can also be a career field. Early in his career the officer rotates between information assignments and other jobs that show him the various operations of the force. Once he reaches the rank of major, he usually will remain in information assignments.[10]

The air force regulation that prescribes how commanders are to pick their information officers directs that the "individual most qualified by Air Force knowledge and experience, aptitude and interest" be selected. Professional education and experience "are highly desirable,"[11] but not essential. To compound the problem, public information is a career field only up to the rank of colonel, so that the top information posts—those of director and deputy director of information—can be filled by someone with no previous public information experience or training. In comparison to the navy, the air force doesn't emphasize a corps of public affairs specialists. Nor is it required that those appointed to the highest positions in the public information field bring a career background to their job.

In the army, the emphasis continues to be on the officer who is a generalist, not a specialist. This has various ramifications for the information officer. He is expected throughout his career to rotate between his warfare speciality—infantry, artillery, or whatever—and his public information speciality.[12] Moreover, a study of army information officers found these specialists are "at a serious disadvantage in the competition to win attendance at senior service schools" where preference is given to the warfare specialties. That, in turn, means that they will suffer when it comes to being promoted.[13]

There is also the phenomenon of the "instant information officer." He is a lieutenant colonel qualified to be promoted who has no experience at all in public information. He is nevertheless "sent to graduate school in journalism and then placed in a key information slot." That has the unintended but real consequence of reducing the chances of the experienced information officer to get "key jobs and promotions and forces him out of the service . . . or out of the program. The entire program suffers from the loss."

The second-rate status of the army information officer is reflected in his not being an equal among staff officers. For instance, in the case of an army corps headquarters, all the staff officers are to be colonels—except for the information officer, who is to be a lieutenant colonel.

Making matters worse still for the information field, commanding officers generally have limited interest in public information and lack knowledge about the field. The study found, "Not having been exposed to information subjects, many commanders view it as a secondary, non-military function."[14]

These different approaches to public information as a career field are in large measure reflected in the backgrounds of the men serving as chiefs and deputy chiefs of information at the time of the field research for this book.

The navy's chief of information was a career public affairs officer—the first ever to head his service's information program. He had attended a predecessor of the Defense Information School, had done graduate work in journalism at the University of Missouri, had gone to the Naval War College, and had held various public affairs jobs at different levels of the navy.[15] His deputy had also made a career of public information. An undergraduate speech major, he had done some graduate work in mass communications and earned a master's degree in international relations. He too had graduated from the Naval War College and had served in public affairs assignments throughout the navy.[16]

In contrast, the army chief of information had been an artillery officer until he was promoted to lieutenant colonel. At that point the army sent him off to complete a bachelor's degree in journalism and to do some graduate work in public relations. His career during the 1960s comprised information assignments, duty as an artillery officer, earning a master's degree in business administration, and attending the Industrial College of the Armed Forces.[17] His deputy had had no formal training in public information before being appointed to the second highest public affairs slot in the army. A West Point graduate with a master's in international relations, he was a career infantry officer whose only prior information experience was a tour as an information officer in Alaska early in his stint with the army.[18]

The head of the air force's information program had pursued a career that focused on flying since graduation from West Point in 1946. He had never held a full-fledged public information job —except as deputy chief of information for the air force for the 10 months before his promotion to the top information position.

Nor did he have any formal training directly related to public information. But he did have a master's in business administration.[19] The deputy was a 1952 graduate of the Naval Academy who had pursued a career involving flying and missiles and had never been in a full-time public information position. He, too, had no formal training related to public information but did hold master's degrees in aeronautical and instrumental engineering.[20]

Although most recent assistant secretaries of public affairs, all civilians, were previously career journalists, none of the chiefs and deputy chiefs of information of the three services, all career officers, had any extensive journalistic experience. The officials interviewed for this study also lacked such experience. Only six had worked for the private media, only three for 10 or more years.

However, most of the officials had spent at least half of their years with the Defense Department working in the public information field. But when it came to formal training directly related to their information jobs, less than half held at least a master's degree in a communications-related field; seven had some relevant training, the others none.

Specific Training in the
Release of Information

This dearth of relevant training is particularly acute in one important area. Although the field research for this study was conducted eight years after Congress passed the Freedom of Information Act, no one in the services or in the office of the secretary of defense could point to a specific, detailed program aimed at teaching Defense officials their obligations to inform the public.

The head of the army's Office for the Freedom of Information said his bureau tries to do as much as it can to make personnel aware of what information is and is not releasable under the law. But, he added, his office—which at the time had a staff of five, including a secretary—does not have the manpower to do an adequate job. In one recent year, that job amounted to about six brief activities, ranging from "presentations" at the army World-Wide Information Officers' Conference to participation in meetings in Colorado "with military and civilian information and media representatives on FoI matters, national and local."[21]

The navy's deputy chief of information said his service also lacked formal programs training officers in the specifics of information release. The navy, he said, deals with the issue at conferences for its information officers and through similar occasional forums.

In the air force this problem is also discussed from time to time at conferences for commanders or information officers and is included as an item in policy pronouncements issued by headquarters in Washington. There are no detailed training programs other than what the Defense Information School (DINFOS) offers.

FoI + DINFOS = ?

The Defense Information School's training on the subject of releasing information is hardly adequate. Even William Donohue, chief of the army's Office for the Freedom of Information, admitted that the school was "just scratching the surface." The military editor of the New York *Times,* Hanson Baldwin, had been much less kind some years earlier. When United States involvement in Vietnam was cresting and the "credibility gap" between the press in Saigon and the military approached chasmlike dimensions, Baldin wrote a piece lashing out at the "distorted, biased and sensational reporting by a few of the younger members of the press and TV corps based on Vietnam"; but he also attacked the Defense Information School.

He found that too many military information officers, particularly those trained in the decade prior to the United States's large-scale involvement in Southeast Asia, "no longer believe that they serve two masters, the executive branch of the government (in the form of their superiors) and the public. This change in attitude and concept is epitomized by the current teachings at the Defense Information School. . . ." Its new concepts, he went on, were well expressed by one of its lecturers whom he quoted as saying: "Our task is to prepare the students for their primary obligation, which will be to the people they work for, the executive branch. The public's right to know is not the controlling factor as far as the individual information officer is concerned."[22]

A few years later, another *Times* reporter, Joseph P. Fried, wrote about the Defense Information School. During a visit to the school in the aftermath of CBS's "The Selling of the Pentagon" he heard the aphorism "maximum disclosure with minimum of delay" expounded in the classroom and defended by students, but he also found heavy emphasis on promotional public relations tactics. An instructor told him: "The military information officer owes his primary allegiance to his commander and through his commander to his service, the President, and their policies. By definition, his interests are different from those of the public and especially any segment of the public that disagrees with Department of Defense policies."

The *Times* reporter experienced information withholding at first hand. "Despite the school's teachings on 'maximum disclosure,' this reporter was denied permission to look at the lesson plans—instructors' outlines—of certain classroom lectures whose content he was interested in but that were given on days he was not visiting the school."[23]

That denial apparently was not unusual. At the suggestion of the chief of the army's Freedom of Information Office, I asked the information school's commandant for his instructors' course outlines dealing with the release of information, particularly those concerning the FoI act and the executive order that governs the classification of information.

Instead of the outlines I received a brief summary written by a member of the school's public affairs department of what is taught on the subject. When I asked again for the lesson plans, there was silence for six weeks. After a reminder, it took another three weeks for a reply from a civilian information specialist: "Unfortunately, the information requested on Instructor's Class Outlines cannot be released."

Without explanation, the outlines dealing with the release of information were not releasable information. Even more interesting, the school that teaches military information specialists how to handle the release of information gave no reason whatever for its action, nor did it advise the requestor that he could appeal the denial if he wished. Yet the Defense Department's own regulation stipulates that both steps are to be taken whenever a request is turned down.[24]

I did appeal. But I made the mistake of addressing the letter by name to the school's commandant, whom I had originally written to three months earlier. He sent me a personal note, pointing out he was in no position to accommodate me. He had retired in the meantime. So I tried again, this time addressing my appeal not to a specific individual, but simply to "commandant," Defense Information School. The new colonel took only two weeks to reply. The lesson plans, requested nearly four months earlier, were at long last enclosed, accompanied by protestations that their release was not legally required. They were being forwarded to maintain the school's "reputation for probity."

What grave or sensitive material did the plans contain? Generally, a succinct description of the FoI act, its amendments, relevant Defense Department policies and regulations, reaffirmations of the maximum-disclosure, minimum-delay slogan, discussion of the "command relationship as a barrier to the release of information," and references to a variety of incidents involving public information problems.

More important than the content of the lesson plans, it turned out, was the time spent on the problems of releasing information: two hours during the school's eight-week course for regular information officers and one hour during its ten-week course for enlisted personnel. Scratching the surface indeed.

It is therefore hardly surprising that a survey of air force information officers found that only 28.0 percent felt they had

been given complete information on the Freedom of Information Act; 57.3 percent said they had received limited information, and 14.7 percent had received none at all. But it is unsettling that 12.0 percent felt unfamiliar with the statute; 67.8
percent felt some familiarity with it, and only 20.2 percent
thought they had a thorough understanding of it.[25]
Perhaps the 1975 amendments toughening the act will result
in more extensive efforts aimed at assuring that Defense personnel understand more fully their responsibilities under the law to
keep the public informed. There seems to be some hope, for
within a year of the amendments, the need for such training was
at last being seriously discussed in the office of the assistant
secretary of defense for public affairs.

While only time will tell whether these discussions will lead
to more than mere regulations that go unenforced, elsewhere in
the Defense Department an attempt to introduce change has
been quietly launched.

Journalism's Best versus
the Navy's Brightest

In 1973, A. M. Rosenthal, managing editor of the *Times,*
spoke at the Naval War College at Newport, Rhode Island
before an audience of carefully selected mid-level career officers
at the school for one year to prepare for some of the highest
military staff and command positions. He raised some uncom-
fortable issues: "There are 7,000 pages in *The Pentagon Papers.*
I think I have read them all. I have come across no discussion
by the military or by the civilian authorities about informing the
public as to what was really happening." And at another point:
"Consider, unhappily consider, My Lai. Not just the massacre,
but the failure to expose and punish until pressure outside the
military became too heavy. . . . Consider the falsification of the
records of the bombing of Cambodia."

He made it clear that he was not blaming solely military men
but also their civilian superiors and the media. When it came to

remedies, he issued the usual call for more sophisticated reporting of military affairs. But he also suggested:

> . . . that no basic decision involving the possibility of war
> be made without the public being told about it, as it is about
> to be made.
> That no public military statement ever be made that is
> untrue.
> That no major political or military error or misdeed
> involving this country be concealed.
> . . . that all this should be part of the philosophy and
> day-to-day practice of our government.

Such an approach, he said, "would have meant that when the
first responsible general officer got word of My Lai he would
have taken it as a matter of duty and honor to open up the whole
case publicly. It would have meant when we bombed Cambodia,
we had said so."[26]

Rosenthal continued in the same vein, critical but comparatively subdued. When David Halberstam spoke before the same
audience, his tone was more biting. One of the younger members
of the American press corps during the early stages of the
Vietnam War, his reporting won him a Pulitzer Prize and pro-
voked a president to try to have him transferred.

Halberstam recalled those early days in Vietnam, during
1962–64, when to the small group of American reporters there,
"you were the heirs of Marshall and Bradley and Eisenhower
and Ridgeway. And we assumed your patriotism and your intelligence." But, he added, "I don't think you gave us comparable
benefit of the doubt."

He pointed to a young general who would rapidly rise to
four-star rank. He disapproved of Halberstam's stories and sent
reports to that effect to the president of the United States—
despite what the general knew to be happening in the field,
despite what his own subordinates told him. Or, Halberstam
said, "I can't tell you how many times when I was a reporter

there, I had my patriotism, my courage or even my manhood challenged." He went on:

> Well, we were just as good as you are as Americans. And the way we honored you! Let me tell you something very bluntly. The next time around you're not going to get, I don't think, as much respect from us, because you're no longer going to be the heirs of Bradley and Marshall and Ridgeway. I'm afraid you're going to be the heirs of Westmoreland, Stilwell, Depew and Lavelle, and the system.[27]

When Halberstam finished with the words, "We're just as good patriots in a very pluralistic, complicated society. We really do our job as well; and some of us in the past have had a great deal of esteem for you and we would hope to see it begin again," he received a standing ovation.

Rosenthal and Halberstam were among a number of prominent journalists who participated in the 1973 military-media conference at the Naval War College. The first had been held in 1972, at the instigation of a vice-admiral, then president of the school, Stansfield Turner. The object of these sessions, Turner told the students at the end of the 1972 conference, was not so much for the officers to dwell on the shortcomings of the press or the way it does its job, "but more on our own inadequacies and on the way in which we carry out our responsibilities in the military-media environment."[28]

This concern in the navy with the relationship between the military and the media—which Turner said needs to be adversarial but "characterized by mutual respect and candor"—has not been limited to the war college. In 1974, it was raised in what is perhaps the navy's most prestigious journal, *The U.S. Naval Institute Proceedings.* Reporting on the war college conferences, the articles said that the officer-students "came to see some of the shortcomings which have contributed little to harmony between the military and the fourth estate over the years." Several examples were cited to support that point:

There has been a clear-cut record of military public affairs mismanagement. Potentially negative stories have been deliberately concealed. Blunder, intentional or unwitting, has made the media suspicious of the military's reliability. . . .
There are people in military public affairs jobs who aren't qualified.
Military seniors ignore the public affairs officer in the management decision-making process.
Too many military officers let the pursuit of career intrude upon crisp, objective thinking and decision making.
The military has not always been truthful in dealing with the media.[29]

In various forms, the message contained in the *Proceedings* article has been carried by members of the navy's information office to other military audiences, among them midshipmen at Annapolis and students at the Industrial College of the Armed Forces.[30] Indeed, within that office, this desire to get naval officers to understand the adversarial role of the American press has been used to justify a program in "public affairs education and training" not only for navy public affairs officers but also senior commanders and others. And the reasons for this need are expressed in in-house communications in blunt language. One memorandum points out naval officers often "do not see themselves as public servants with a real, continuing responsibility to account for their actions to the public, but rather [as] a somewhat elitist group requiring support from the public." The writer, a career public affairs officer with a doctorate in mass communications who headed the program planning division in the navy's Office of Information, continues:

The average officer's instinct is to ignore the media and get on with the job and tell the story, if he has to, afterward. I feel the naval officer's way to handle the state of personal uncertainty about public affairs is to cover the uncertainty with extra positiveness, to crush arguments that might aggravate uncertainty before they are heard. . . .
The average naval officer does not understand or appreciate

the role of the free press and the traditions of the press corps of this country. They want to believe the press should play as team members, not as adversaries to government. They view the function of public affairs as tangent to, not as integral part of, their jobs and the operations and administrative requirements of the institutions.[31]

Inferior Information Officers
and Misguided Commanders

The navy's is not alone in its concern with educating its public affairs specialists and its other officers to ensure that they understand the role of the media in the American political system and their responsibilities as public officials to keep the public informed. Although the other two services and the office of the assistant secretary for public affairs seem less concerned, many of the interviewed officials and correspondents mentioned this need.

Again and again, in reply to one or another of the questions that guided this exploratory study and that were discussed in this and the preceding chapter, the reporters and information specialists interviewed unexpectedly brought out two factors which need to be made explicit.

First, they pinpointed the commanding officer, other superiors, or simply "pressure from above." Most of the officials in one way or another indicated that if negative information is manipulated, it is likely to happen because those in charge either feel no obligation to release it, are not aware that there are legal limits restricting what they can withhold, or because they are afflicted by the "proud-father syndrome" which holds that the affairs of the unit under the officer's control are no one's concern but his. Not all of the officials felt equally strongly about the matter; some only touched on it, but most mentioned it more often, frequently at some length and with considerable fervor.

So did a¹l of the reporters. However, unlike the officials—who tended to pinpoint commanding officers as a likely cause when bad news is manipulated—the journalists were less specific, frequently lumping the phenomenon under the label of "pressure from above." And the intensity with which the reporters perceived the commander as a likely stumbling block to the flow of unfavorable news varied. But more than half indicated that pressure from above was a significant factor in the handling of untoward information, usually in connection with what they saw as the limited utility of public information officers who must do as they are told by higher-ranking superiors.

That the information officer's utility is limited by his boss's beck and call is beyond doubt—even if the public affairs specialist has stars emboidered on his epaulets. As Phil Goulding, the Pentagon's former assistant secretary for public affairs, put it, no matter how well-intentioned the information officer is when it comes to getting the negative story out, he "too often lacks clout to make his position stick." That, he adds, holds true even for the rear admirals and major generals who run the information operations of the military services.[32]

The second unexpected factor that emerged—perhaps because it is so obvious—was simply the unqualified or incompetent public information officer. He is the information officer who does not understand the role of the press, who is not aware that the function of governmental public information is basically different from corporate PR, or who is not conversant with the legal limits of how much information the government can withhold. He was singled out by only about half of the officials as a factor in the manipulation of negative news. However, if one adds to the definition of unqualified information officers the inability to persuade the commander to release bad news and, if that fails, to find ways to circumvent him—then most officials see the incompetent public affairs officer as a likely cause for the manipulation of negative information.

Of the journalists, only three felt the incompetent information officer was a factor. That does not mean that they felt most public information specialists are qualified. They simply felt that their role is so circumscribed and restricted that they do not matter significantly in the information-handling process.

It is not very difficult to find examples of the disastrous effect the imperious commander and the impotent public affairs officer can have on the flow of information. A 1964 report to the assistant secretary of defense for public affairs documents as case in print. Early that year bloody riots broke out in the Panama Canal Zone over the terms of the Canal Treaty. Precipitated by a dispute over the way a U.S. flag was flown in the zone —not flanked by Panama's—American troops and Panamanians clashed. More than two dozen persons were killed, including four U.S. soldiers, and scores were wounded. The clashes led to a break of diplomatic relations between the two countries. With the outbreak of the violence, control over the Canal Zone shifted to the commander of the U.S. Southern Command, Lt. Gen. Andrew P. O'Meara. His public affairs policy, an emissary dispatched by the assistant secretary for public affairs would subsequently find, "was short-sighted and defensive."

For instance, during the first days of the rioting, O'Meara imposed "a virtual news blackout" in the zone. As Assistant Secretary Arthur Sylvester was told: "Reporters and photographers were barred outright from areas of action or hindered in their movement by commanders on the ground. The pretext given them was that their safety could not be guaranteed." The radio and television stations operated by the Southern Command in the zone were "ordered not to mention the riots in newscasts. The decision to withhold news from the local population was made by [O'Meara] personnally." The result? "The U.S. story was not told promptly and completely so that it could counter untruths published by the Panamanian press."

Another result of that policy, Sylvester learned, was the worldwide circulation of stories that protrayed the United States as the aggressor. Written by Panamanian nationals working as stringers for the wire services, these stories had U.S. troops crouching behind tanks in the Canal Zone and firing machine guns across the boundary into Panama. They were not officially denied for nearly three days, when the general had his first and only meeting with the press.

One reason the stories about the use of machine guns and

tanks circulated for so long was the failure of the Southern Command to analyze them carefully and to respond to them promptly. Indeed, the denial was initially made on a "background basis." But in addition, the public information officer of the Southern Command was not advised of how critical the situation was until the violence was at its peak. Worse still, the information officials were excluded from the battle staff through which O'Meara directed his operations. They did not even have a direct phone line to that staff. Consequently, the information officials were severely hindered in rounding up information they could distribute to the media. And O'Meara would not permit any one besides himself to approve the release of information. "At times, the [public affairs officer] had to wait at least five hours before he could see [O'Meara] and get the proposed announcements cleared."

All this, Sylvester was told, "gave the Panamanians an uncontested propaganda advantage. . . . The U.S. story—particularly that part which denied the use of machine guns and tanks—was told too late to counter the Panamanians' propaganda advantage or to reverse world opinion."[33]

Thus, if "bad" news is manipulated, it's neither the "military mind" nor the fearful subordinate who are to be blamed. Instead, the more likely culprit is an official who feels no genuine responsibility to inform the public—perhaps an overly secretive commander—or a less than effective public information officer —or perhaps both.

8

The Gatekeepers:
Few and Friendly

~~~~~~~~~~~~~~~~~~~~~~~~~~

The whole project had been very hush-hush. Although the
United States had detonated the nuclear devices in the upper
atmosphere six months earlier, the tests were still supposed to
be secret. Yet the military editor of the New York *Times* had
known of them ever since they occurred—indeed, he had been
aware of them since long before they were even set off.

But Hanson Baldwin and his newspaper held up pretest publication because Pentagon officials feared that premature publicity might cause the blasts to be cancelled. In deference to Defense Department requests, posttest publication was also
delayed. Only now, six months after the explosions, only when
it appeared that the department itself might release some information about the tests, was the story published. And then only
after notifying the Pentagon and the White House in advance
that the story would be run.

That happened in 1959.[1] Four years later, the journalistic
fraternity was still embroiled in the debate over the claim by
Arthur Sylvester, then the assistant secretary of defense for
public affairs, of the government's "right to lie." Lester Markel,
at the time the Sunday editor of the *Times*, was troubled by

journalists' arguments that the news should be printed no matter what. That line of thinking, in Markel's view, "implies that there are no other considerations and no responsibilities other than the stark pursuit of the facts. But there *are* other elements involved, notably that of the 'national interest.' " Stressing that the cold war was on, he went on to echo President Kennedy: "Newspapers should recognize that it is not enough, in these critical days, to ask: Is it news? They must also ask: Is it in the national interest?"[2]

Harrison Salisbury, also with the *Times,* wrote a series of articles in late 1966 from North Vietnam. They contradicted the American claim that bombings in the north had been limited to military targets. Eventually, the U.S. government acknowledged that these targets included military installations in Hanoi and that some civilian areas may have been hit accidentally. When Salisbury returned to the United States, he found that among the critics of his widely distributed and debated reports was his newspaper's military editor, "who was overheard muttering unpleasantries about Salisbury through the halls of the *Times.* "[3]

Meanwhile, in the Pentagon, "each of the Salisbury pieces was duplicated and distributed within the government for line-by-line analysis." On the basis of the information the Defense Department had, the government's assessment differed considerably from what Salisbury claimed to have seen in North Vietnam. And, writes the man who was assistant secretary of defense for public affairs at the time, "the Pentagon press was largely sympathetic" with the government's position.[4]

Just how sympathetic and cooperative the Pentagon press corps can be is illustrated by a story that appeared in the Washington *Post* a year later. Although the *Post* had a regular correspondent covering the Defense Department, in the fall of 1967 it found itself in the curious position of having to use wire service copy saying that "certain U.S. officials were deeply concerned" that Cambodia's port of Sinanoukville might become a source of military supplies for the North Vietnamese and the South Vietnamese National Liberation Front.

The *Post's* regular Pentagon correspondent was apparently not as regular as some of the others. Consequently, he was not invited to a private, off-the-record dinner with General William C. Westmoreland at the Washington home of the Baltimore *Sun's* military writer. Others at the dinner included the Pentagon correspondents of the AP, UPI, *Times, Christian Science Monitor,* Washington *Star, Wall Street Journal,* and Los Angeles *Times.*

"It was agreed at the dinner [held November 17, 1967] that they would publish the Westmoreland information November 24. There also seems to have been some agreement as to how and what would be said," reported Seymour Hersh, himself an ex-AP Pentagon correspondent. He went on to quote stories about the Sihanoukville fears that appeared in the *Star,* the *Times,* and were carried by the Associated Press, all strikingly similar. Hersh further reported that "such meetings have been a commonplace for years."[5]

As the Vietnam War continued, the Pentagon press corps became the object of some scrutiny. It emerged that certain Defense correspondents who "accept the assumptions of the military" were asked to write articles for military journals and were honored with awards by a reserve army detachment composed of journalists. And ranking media executives were invited for cruises aboard navy aircraft carriers to Hawaii.[6]

In the winter of 1970, in a *Columbia Journalism Review* issue on the lessons the media should have learned from the Vietnam War, Jules Witcover, who has covered the Pentagon himself, wrote about the Washington's press corps' failure in reporting the conflict. They had done "a highly professional job" of "reporting what the government said" but had fallen down "finding out whether it was true, and assessing whether the policy worked." Zeroing in on the Pentagon correspondents, Witcover said that "as the doubts of young American reporters in Vietnam were trickling home in their dispatches, older news hands at the Pentagon were likely to dismiss them as the product of the inexperienced."[7]

Neil Sheehan, a Pulitzer Prize winner who covered the Pentagon for the *Times* in the mid-1960s but who is better known for obtaining the Pentagon Papers, draws a more specific lesson for the media from the escapades of Lt. Cmdr. Marcus Arnheiter and the U.S.S. *Vance*. Sheehan writes that the "time-honored newspaper techniques of scribbling a few details in a notebook, hustling them into something readable on a typewriter, casting the words into a column and then rushing on to another story the next day, was appropriate to policebeat reporting in Chicago in the 1920's. It is an anachronism today." He adds that every journalist knows that the consequence of this approach "is the daily publication of falsehood and bias in favor of those who know best how to exploit its weakness."[8]

Perhaps the harshest criticism of the press's performance came from Clark R. Mollenhoff, Pulitzer Prize-winning chief of the Des Moines *Register*'s Washington bureau. He criticized the acceptance of the "self-serving declarations of the Defense Secretary were accepted as truths, even when they were clearly contradicted by a body of testimony and documentation." This was done because only "a few of the Pentagon reporters will fight the system and risk the cold and uncooperative treatment handed out to those who are regarded as 'unfriendly' or 'unsympathetic' to the civilian power structure."[9]

There are many examples of that "cold and uncooperative treatment." In 1968 James Phillips, in a special *Congressional Quarterly* report, explained how some Pentagon officials thought $10 billion could be trimmed from the Defense Department's $70 billion budget. One of the ways Defense officials responded to Phillips's report was to circulate the document "through various departments as a part of their inquiry into possible 'security leaks,' causing many officials to cut off their contacts with Phillips."

On another occasion in 1968, after the *Times* had disclosed that the American commander in Vietnam, General Westmoreland, had requested another 206,000 troops, one military reporter says that for several months the Joint Chiefs of Staff would not "even let me in the door, not even on routine matters." He said he had a good source in that office whom he saw regularly, but this source "literally slammed the door in my face the last time I went to see him. And neither he nor I had anything to do with the leak."[10]

An appraisal by two journalists buttresses what these examples suggest about the relationship between Pentagon officials and reporters. In their analysis of stories written by Pentagon correspondents in one month in 1973, the two journalists found that of 155 stories, 89 "had as their primary basis the public pronouncements of senior military officials or their spokesmen." "Another 33 stories [were] based on the say-so of anonymous sources." That means, they concluded, that the "total number of stories devoted mainly to views of or information from the military hierarchy climbs to 122—more than 75 per cent of the copy written by Pentagon regulars during the thirty days in question".[11]

This reluctance to dig up the facts may not be unusual. Another study indicates that three-fourths of the stories by State Department correspondents were also based on similar official sources of information; only a fourth were the result of enterprising reporting.[12]

Reporters and Officials on
Reporters versus Officials

But as every college freshman knows, theoretically at least the American media is to be more than a mere transmission channel that forwards information from government to governed, from the Pentagon to the public. The media have been called the responsible adversary of government,[13] the fourth branch that checks whether the other three branches are checking on each other.[14] Even before the reenactment in living color of Bob Woodward's and Carl Bernstein's Watergate reportage, other students of American government described the media as "remarkably vigorous in the pursuit of 'inside stories';[15] as the "wielder of the spotlight that bathes government in luxuriating publicity";[16] one claimed that "the brashness of American newspapermen in ferreting out information is legendary. . . ."[17]

There are dissenters from such assessments,[18] including the political scientist Dan D. Nimmo. After a long look at government information officers and reporters in Washington, Nimmo concluded that the relationship between the two has increasingly become more cozy. He notes that journalists, officials, and public information specialists are perhaps all "assuming 'responsible leadership' to mean an agreement between government and press leaders that certain matters can be publicized in the 'national interest' while others must remain unrevealed, hidden or overlooked."[19]

Does excessive compatibility lead to news manipulation? Of the Pentagon correspondents,* only one flatly rejected the notion that news manipulation succeeds because the press doesn't push hard enough. The power of the media is vastly overrated, said the Associated Press veteran at the Pentagon, Fred Hoffman. "If they don't want to talk, they can keep the lid on," he explained, particularly if only a few top officials are in the know. This is especially true when "touchy, diplomatic situations" are involved, and when there is pressure from the White House. Over time, he said, it is nevertheless likely that some of the information will leak, "but they can make it so tough you can get only a piece or two or you get it too late."

As reporters see it, there are too few of them covering an incredibly complex agency in which public interest wanes as the sabres are sheathed. Kane of *Time* called the Pentagon press

---

*It will be recalled that of the ten newsmen interviewed, eight were from among the 10 to 12 who cover the Pentagon on a regular basis for the general circulation media as of mid-1974. It was impossible to pinpoint the number of regular, general media correspondents more precisely than that. The newsmen as well as the interviewed officials disagreed when asked to specify the exact number. For instance, one older correspondent was nominally assigned full-time to the Defense Department. However, his full-time colleagues pointed out that he no longer spent most of his time pursuing the beat. In view of such definitional problems, it was decided to use the figure of 10 to 12.

corps "as good as any crew in town." However, "Defense officials can get away with withholding and playing down stories
simply because there are not enough guys who keep them honest." Moreover, he added, the end of the Vietnam War brought
the usual public indifference toward the military, resulting in
less coverage.

Half of the journalists, however, were willing to assign at least
some of the blame for news not getting out to the lack of
reportorial persistence. But they, too, pointed to a variety of
other contributing factors. "There are guys, I'm sure, who cover
the Pentagon and who take on its ways, who share its ideology,"
said the *Post*'s Pentagon correspondent, Michael Getler. But he
added that the Defense Department "is the toughest agency to
cover" in Washington. A larger problem still, he felt, is the small
number of reporters who cover military affairs on a full-time
basis and the limited importance most news organizations attach to the military when no shots are being fired.

John Finney of the *Times* deemed it a fair generalization that
lack of persistence helps the Pentagon withhold or distort information. He too, however, pointed to the few reporters who
cover the department for the general media. Making matters
even worse, too many of them stay too close to the Pentagon.
Important stories are not ready-made for the press, he said—
Defense correspondents need to spend as much time on Capitol
Hill as at the Pentagon to dig up all relevant information.

Steinhauser of the *Armed Forces Journal* was toughest on his
brethren. Only two or three work hard to dig up information,
he said. "The press is lazy and arrogant. They won't educate
themselves and let [Defense information officials] manipulate
them." Most of the Pentagon correspondents, he said, expect to
be provided with information because "of who they are." "They
want answers put on a platter." The standard press refrain,
according to Steinhauser, is: "I can't read all that crap—tell me
what it says"—an attitude that makes it possible for the information officers to exploit them.

Although Steinhauser was by far the most outspoken on the
subject, some of the other newsmen, when pressed to pass judg-

ment, agreed that of the 10 to 12 full-time reporters representing the general media at the Pentagon, only half dig hard and persistently. But they emphasized that those who do not dig hard or persistently may have little or no choice. Some, at least, are under constant deadline pressure, particularly those working for the wire services and daily newspapers. They see their first obligation as the reporting of the never-ending flow of official statements, announcements, and speeches. They often compete to be first to get the information in print or on the air. Little time is left to crosscheck the veracity of an official claim with their own sources.

In sum, most of the interviewed Pentagon correspondents agree that the journalist's diligence is a factor when news is withheld or distorted. But they were divided on the reasons why reporters fail. Laziness and the lack of an adequate Pentagon press force were mentioned, but half of the journalists thought a combination of the two elements was at work: basically, that there aren't enough reporters with hard noses.*

Of the officials regularly involved in the handling of information, a third said that the lack of journalistic persistence is not a factor in news withholding or distortion.

The navy's deputy chief of information, Captain Cooney, had not found many overly sympathetic reporters among the regulars. He agreed, though, that some push harder to get the com-

---

*A simple comparison puts this concern with the size of the regular Pentagon press corps into stark perspective. As noted, there are only about a dozen regulars at Defense for the general circulation media, 20 to 24 when correspondents for such special publications as trade journals and periodicals aimed mainly at military audiences are added. In contrast, the New York *Times* city desk alone has a staff of approximately 200 to cover the news in and around New York City—not to mention the more than four dozen working for the paper's sports editor and the five dozen who work for the financial news editor.[20]

Additional figures also show that this small number of regulars is neither a new nor a temporary phenomenon. In 1965, there were 18 reporters from the general media covering the Defense Department on a "full-time or near full-time basis" plus "eleven from the trade."[21]

plete story than others. Cooney also thought that their small number is a real handicap, a situation that he found particularly worrisome because the number of professional military writers across the United States is small. Including the Pentagon regulars, he estimated it at perhaps 25.

Lieutenant Colonel Kelly, chief of the air force information office's Operations Forces Branch, termed the notion that newsmen are not persistent enough as "ridiculous." "There are lazy guys," he said, "but they don't last."

A senior civilian public information specialist in the office of the assistant secretary for public affairs did see bad reporting as a problem. He said the correspondents fail to follow up on leads, usually because they do not have the time. A "responsible adversary relationship" between the press and the Pentagon is essential, he said because it is naive to think that government officials will always tell all they know: "It doesn't serve the public interest to have supine reporters telling only what officials think the public needs to know."

Most of the other officials felt that the lack of persistence was only an occasional factor in the manipulation of information. Capt. Ralph L. Slawson, head of the press division in the office of the assistant secretary of defense for public affairs, cautioned that his judgment might be biased: "I still maintain a personal and professional feeling that the newspaper reporter, with all his warts, is a pretty holy guy in our system—despite the pummeling they've given me from time to time." Nevertheless, he has seen some changes of late in the reporters covering the Defense Department. During the latter stages of the Vietnam War, "they were tough, perceptive, inventive, hard-hitting, and often a pain in the ass." That did not bother him because in response he would "blow some steam in their direction." With the end of the war, however, he has seen that adversarial relationship fade. There are still some very aggressive correspondents at the Pentagon, Slawson said, but their number is declining.

A few officials saw the problem from a somewhat different angle. They stressed that the Defense regulars do not get out of the capital often enough and faulted local reporters outside of

Washington who are nowhere near as persistent and aggressive as those covering the Pentagon.

The chief of the Air Force's public information division, Col. Robert Hermann, complained that the regulars stick too close to Washington. Media owners and publishers, he said, "have become mesmerized with the Washington dateline. They now have Pentagon correspondents while they used to have military affairs writers" who reported on the armed forces by constantly traveling to military installations and covering activities around the country and the world. He said: "If there is that genuine interest in covering the military, they ought to spend a lot more time where it happens."

Among those criticizing unaggressive local reporters was Capt. Fred Ellis, public affairs officer for the navy's Materiel Command, who said there is the reporter "who won't settle for the release or for what you say. They are the best. You can't B.S. them. And if you do, they're going to make you look sick." But Ellis added, the local media, particularly in "big navy towns" like Norfolk or San Diego, rarely knock his service.

Other data support these views. All those interviewed, even the Defense correspondents, acknowledged they do little traveling to cover the far-flung department. And a study examining the relationships between air force information officers stationed around the country and the journalists with whom they deal offers more evidence. It found, for example, that of the 87 journalists outside of Washington who participated, nearly two-thirds either were satisfied or very satisfied with the performance of the information officer with whom they dealt. Of the 75 information officers questioned, nearly 90 percent were either satisfied or very satisfied with the performance of the reporters. Only one information specialist was very dissatisfied.

Moreover, when the journalists were asked whether they could rely on the information officer with whom they dealt to give them complete and accurate responses, three-fourths said, yes, most of the time. Three-fourths of officers said that they could rely on the journalists to report news of their organization accurately most of the time.

These "data strongly suggest," the study concluded, "that journalists and information officers agree on important issues far more than they disagree. This finding indicates that the characterization of the interaction process as being one of adversarity may be overstated." Indeed, "far more respondents appeared to opt for a cooperative and conciliatory media-government relationship" than a conflict-ridden one.[22]

In other words, some correspondents, if not in bed with the Pentagon's brass, are far too friendly with them. Certainly many local reporters are too soft on the military. But the greater problem is the small number of Defense regulars. Deadline pressure often leaves them no choice but to transmit official prouncements without adequate scrutiny. They haven't the time nor the resources to dip deeply enough or travel far enough to get the complete story.

9

Contours of
a Pattern

Numerous examples in this study offer ample proof that the Department of Defense manipulates information in a variety of ways. Although no large public organization, particularly the military, can make all information about its current activities available, a variety of incidents in recent years indicates that the Pentagon's restrictive information practices have exceeded such legitimate withholding again and again.

It is easy to show *how* the Pentagon handles bad news; *why* they do so is a much more complex problem. Although the government-media relationship has been examined extensively, most studies have focused on the flow of positive information between government and the press and have largely ignored the processing of bad news within public organizations. And even less is known about the handling of such information within organizations that possess characteristics unique to the military.

Consequently, drawing on material about public administration, military organizations, and mass communications, eight plausible—albeit competing—factors were chosen, at the outset of this study, as possible reasons for the Pentagon's management of public information.

These variables turned out to differ considerably in their relevance. Some were extremely significant, others of only limited importance. Moreover, two completely unanticipated but extremely important factors emerged.

In Summary: The "Whys" of Public Information Policies

1. The Pentagon's concern for outside support of its policies appears to play at least a moderate role in the handling of bad news. Information that might adversely affect a defense policy or program may be withheld or distorted.

2. The extensive secrecy that permeates the Pentagon exerts a similar moderate influence. If bad news threatens to interfere with the pursuit of that holy but elusive ghost, national security, then it may be manipulated.

3. The department's emphasis on self-serving public relations does not seem to cause officials to manipulate information to any great extent.

4. Similarly, the data simply do not support the oft-repeated allegation that information officers' vested interest in releasing positive information leads them to suppress bad news. However, the role of the public information specialist is indeed significant in other ways. Withholding or distortion of news often occurs because of Pentagon-imposed restrictions that govern much of what the information officer can or cannot release. The quality and competence of his work also has a direct bearing on the dissemination of news. An information officer who does not fully understand the role of the press in the American political system, or is not aware that governmental public information functions differ from corporate PR, may distort bad news.

5. Support for the idea that news manipulation results from the career officer's obsession with secrecy proved nonexistant. There is no indication that the military's ideology affects the way unfavorable news is handled. But another characteristic of military organizations does seem to play a very significant role:

the commanding officer. Although his command authority has shrunk somewhat in recent decades, primarily because the impact of technology has caused specialists to share some of that authority, the commanding officer remains the focal point in an authority structure that emphasizes hierarchy to ensure uniform, central direction in combat situations.[1] The commander —or other heads of major organizational units—is a significant factor in how bad news is handled. If he is afflicted by the "proud-father-syndrome," believing that anything negative about his unit is his business only, then it is very likely that such information will be distorted or suppressed.

6. Very limited support emerged for the notion that news is manipulated because fearful subordinates are afraid to pass the information upward to those who can release it. Indeed, the evidence suggests that the opposite is true: the more significant the bad news, the less likely that subordinates can withhold it from their superiors.

7. Officials who do not feel obligated to keep the public fully informed turned out to be a significant factor. If these officials —not only commanders and information officers but also privates, sergeants, lieutenants, captains, and civil servants—do not believe that there are limits to what the government can conceal, then news is likely to be withheld or distorted.

8. Limited support exists for the notion that the manipulation of "blackeye" stories is due to an excessively harmonious relationship between reporters and defense officials. News manipulation may occasionally occur because journalists are too supportive of military officials and fail to dig deeply enough in researching a story. However, the evidence suggests rather strongly that the problem is not so much that the reporters' noses aren't hard enough as that there are too few such noses.

Although is is analytically useful to list these factors individually, it is unrealistic to conclude that the solo performance of any one variable alone results in news manipulation. A combination of these variables, some more directly than others, is involved when bad news is manipulated. Some appear to be environmental variables which set the stage, whereas the others are more specific variables, motivating the individuals involved in the handling of negative information. For example, the emphasis the Defense Department places on positive self-serving publicity appears to be an environmental variable of only limited significance. However, as a result of the emphasis on positive PR, a variety of restrictions are imposed on information officers. And these restrictions constitute a variable of considerable significance. Similarly, unfavorable news is often manipulated because the involved officials generally do not feel obligated to keep the public informed. That, in turn, manifests itself more specifically through commanding officers who are not fully aware of their responsibilities as public officials to release unrestricted information.

These environmental factors provide a background for the more significant variables affecting individual behavior. For example, on rare occasions news manipulation may occur because of fearful subordinates. It is much more likely to happen, however, because incompetent information specialists handle the story. And even if the information officer is competent, his commander—whose orders he must obey and who controls his career through performance ratings—may not care to inform the public. Such manipulation may succeed because some of the Pentagon press corps embraces the military a bit too passionately. However, such attempts are more likely to succeed simply because there are too few journalists regularly covering the agency.

A Ready Illustration.

Most of these variables were all too clearly operating in the handling of My Lai.

All the Americal Division information specialists who appeared before the Peers inquiry agreed that they saw their jobs primarily in terms of generating favorable information. Even some of the questions by panel members indicate that they, too, expect army information officers to report good news only.

Information concerning My Lai was restricted until early 1975, almost seven years after the incident occurred, readily exemplifying the secrecy syndrome.

The concern with guarding information that runs counter to policy is perhaps best illustrated by the way pictures were treated that showed Americal Division troops engaged in activities that were not "in keeping with the standards." They were neither enlarged nor distributed.

The general lack of a sense of obligation to inform the public fully is all too clearly reflected in the behavior of figures ranging from the secretary of defense to the soldiers and officers on the scene at Son My.

Information personnel who say that they did not have an inkling for over a year of a massacre committed by troops of their own division illustrate the problem of incompetence. Yet, a G.I. belonging to a different division, who had neither attended the Defense Information School nor received civilian training or experience in information handling, managed to find out on his own within weeks what had happened at My Lai.

The same holds true for the commanding officers. The commander of the task force that operated at My Lai made it clear that the army reporter was not to worry about the disparity between the high body count and the few weapons captured. And the Americal Division's commanding general, according to the Peers inquiry, seems to have done everything but make public what had occurred at Son My. Furthermore, even if the Americal's information specialists wanted to make the news of My Lai public, it appears that higher headquarters would have blue-penciled it.

Finally, none of the American reporters who were in Vietnam at the time appear to have been anywhere near My Lai when the massacre occurred or shortly afterward. When the action later shifted to the United States, journalists working for the mass media did not actively pursue the story. One reporter who knew a good deal about it did not want to embarrass the army. When a freelance writer was tipped off, however, he managed to obtain the details by traveling outside Washington to locate key individuals, which most regular correspondents assigned to the Pentagon rarely do.

Some Tentative Suggestions

A number of steps that would curtail the manipulation of bad news readily suggest themselves. Given the exploratory nature of this book, they can only be recommended cautiously; but to take no action at all would be like refusing a cancer victim chemotherapy because the disease's precise cause has not yet been discovered.

First, the environmental variables. If the Defense Department is to eliminate or at least reduce news manipulation, it will have to shift its emphasis from positive publicity—patterned after the model of corporate public relations—to a policy of more straightforward, less self-serving public information. It is unlikely, however, that the department will make this shift without support and, if necessary, pressure from its political environment. Above all, the Pentagon can make this move only with the backing and encouragement of the president, not to mention precedents set by him. Such a shift is critical if Defense officials generally are to become more aware of their responsibilities to inform the public as fully as the law requires. Once such an awareness is aroused, it would be necessary for the secretary of defense, the secretaries of the various services, as well as the uniformed military leadership to make clear through explicit—and enforceable—directives that the Pentagon's information policy really is "maximum disclosure with minimum delay."

As far as the climate of secrecy is concerned, it will hardly be tempered until some genuine steps are taken to bring under control a system that has generated nearly 2,300 stacks of classified documents, each as high as the Washington Monument, and that punishes no one for overclassification.

In terms of security and policy review, the present system makes it all too easy to withhold or play down negative but releasable information. It is one thing to protect policy from rhetorical attacks by carping subordinates. It is quite another thing, however, to review and censor factual material that does not support courses of action to which the department has committed itself. It is, of course, impossible to differentiate clearly between the two. But the current policy and security review system makes abuses likely. It would seem that the World War II system of voluntary censorship—which completely segregated public relations activities from review procedures—might be used profitably as a model for contemporary policy review.

That does not mean to suggest that the Defense Department should be authorized to engage in peacetime censorship, voluntary or otherwise. It is to say, however, that policy and security review should be removed entirely from public relations channels. It should be handled by separate offices staffed primarily with experienced journalists well versed in the provisions of the Freedom of Information Act; prepared to make the difficult judgments involved in releasing accurate, documented, unclassified information—*even if it is not supportive of an important policy or program*—and willing to limit policy and security review to unsubstantiated polemics by Pentagon personnel against an officially promulgated Defense Department position.

Second, there are those factors which are linked more directly to the manipulation of bad news. A reappraisal of the role of the commanding officer and the information specialist—especially vis à vis their responsibility to the public—seems crucial to improving the Pentagon's information practices.

The navy has begun special training and education for personnel headed for command positions. Eventually, such educational efforts should start at the service academies, traditionally the source of America's top military officers, and continue at schools attended by those officers deemed suitable for posts of extensive authority. To reach those now in command positions, special media-military relations seminars, patterned after those initiated at the Naval War College, should be held at the various regular conferences commanders of the different services now attend.

Similar training is also necessary to upgrade the quality and competence of information specialists. Again, the first step might be to include such training at the various regular conferences these officers have to attend. A review of the training provided by the Defense Information School—particularly in the area of public information handling and release—also seems necessary to assure that those information specialists who go through its programs are, indeed, adequately trained.

Beyond that, the public information speciality within each service must be upgraded to be on a par with other career specializations. Eventually, information officers must have the same opportunities for promotion afforded other specialists. Their rank will have to be equal to that of other staff officers; they will have to be evaluated not solely on the basis of whether they please their commanding officer but also on the basis of competence. Changes must be introduced so that only career information specialists can attain the most senior positions in the public information field.

In addition, there must be an urgent examination of the feasibility of establishing in each service a corps of experts who specialize exclusively in handling public information. Mainly media-relations specialists, they would not be involved in the usual PR chores of turning out good-news-only house organs or creating public support for various Pentagon policies.[2]

On a broader scale, beyond the scope of the Defense Department, the American public administration community must consider whether the time has come to play a more significant role in the training of public information personnel working for government. For example, it might prove feasible for a public administration program to combine its talents with a journalism school to create a special program at the master's degree level. It would be specifically aimed at training public information–media relations specialists who plan to work in government. Such a public-administration sponsored program hopefully would not continue the all-too-pervasive pattern of eliminating from the field of public administration one of the largest public organizations in the nation—the American military—but would instead make a deliberate effort to attract the Pentagon's public information specialists.

Less promising than attempts to educate commanders and information officers is the possibility of reducing the array of restrictions that govern so much of what the military information specialist can do. It is, of course, possible that these restrictions will diminish as a result of internal pressures if and when the competence of information officers is upgraded. A change is more likely to happen, however, when the Pentagon's heavy emphasis on selfserving publicity is itself sharply reduced.

To help make sure that these circumscriptions on information officers do not exceed the law, a very small number of senior officials should be specially designated within each service and in the office of the secretary of defense. Their job would be to enforce—not merely suggest—adherence to the Freedom of Information Act. Indeed, following the lead set by the Department of Health, Education, and Welfare, these should be the only officials permitted to deny requests for information.

Finally, there is the press. As a first step, the media might want to review the performance of its reporters now at the Pentagon, perhaps transferring some correspondents too supportive of the department and others too cavalier in their coverage. The media might find that a good investigative reporter, once he or she has become throughly acquainted with the Defense Department, will generate news at least as fit to be printed as that provided by press conferences and official blue tops. While the assignment of 10 to 12 such investigative reporters to the department—not a likely event if for no other reason than their scarcity—would probably result in less successful news manipulation, the vastness and complexity of the Pentagon would limit even their effectiveness.

However, the quickest, most effective way to reduce news management—but also one of the least likely—would be to triple or quadruple the number of regulars at the Pentagon. This would be particularly effective if these reporters were free to travel extensively outside of Washington. As the manager of the

Washington bureau of United Press International told the
American Society of Newspaper Editors in 1972:

> . . . the campaign against secrecy in government basically
> must be carried on by succeeding ranks of skilled reporters.
> They must steep themselves in their subject; they must be
> aggressive while also winning the confidence of their sources.
> And they must be backed up by editors who understand that
> this kind of reporting takes time and superior talent, and are
> willing to pay for it. And who aren't satisfied with a superfi-
> cial job.[3]

Since then, UPI has reduced its Pentagon correspondents from
two to one. So did the Associated Press. And others.

Notes

CHAPTER 1

1. Seymour M. Hersh, *My Lai 4* (New York: Random House, 1970), pp. 128–29.
2. U. S. Department of the Army, *Report of the Department of the Army Review of the Preliminary Investigations into the My Lai Incident* (The Peers inquiry), "The Report of the Investigation" (14 March 1970), 1:1/14.
3. Seymour Hersh, *Cover-Up* (New York: Random House, 1972), pp. 246–47.
4. The account of the press conference is based on Hersh, *Cover-Up*, pp. 248–53.
5. Army, *Peers Inquiry*, 1:2/4.
6. Hersh, *Cover-Up*, passim.
7. Carole Fader, "The Freedom of Information Act and the Media," *Freedom of Information Center Report No. 303* (Columbia, Mo.: University of Missouri, School of Journalism, May 1973), p. 4.
8. Army, *Peers Inquiry*, 1:2/2, 2/3.
9. Ibid., 2:22, testimony of Jay A. Roberts. Most of the other testimony referred to in the remainder of this chapter comes from volume 2 of the *Peers Inquiry*. That volume is divided into separate sections, each containing the testimony of individual witnesses. The material referred to in the following pages—unless otherwise

indicated—can be found in volume 2 under the name of the person
to whom it is attributed here.

10. Ibid., Exhibit M-23.
11. Ibid., Exhibit M-17.
12. Ibid., Exhibit M-58.
13. Ibid., Exhibit M-61.
14. Ibid., "Communiqué Describes Quang Ngai Massacre."
15. Ibid., 1:2/3.
16. Ibid., 1:8/5–8/6.
17. Lt. Col. Hugh M. Waite, chief, news branch, public information
    division, office of the chief of information, U. S. army, to J. Arthur
    Heise, 23 May 1975.
18. Army, *Peers Inquiry,* 1:9/11.
19. Testimony of John W. Moody in *U.S.* v. *Henderson* (CM 428589,
    21:5234–39).
20. Army, *Peers Inquiry,* 1:1/7–1/11.
21. Hersh, *My Lai 4,* p. 130. See pp. 103–43 for a detailed account of
    how the information about My Lai 4 was originally brought to
    light.
22. Ibid., p. 132.
23. For the most detailed account of how Hersh managed to do so, see
    Joe Eszterhas, "The Reporter Who Broke the My Lai Massacre,
    the Secret Bombing of Cambodia and the CIA Domestic Spying
    Stories," *Rolling Stone,* 10 April 1975, pp. 48–81.
24. Hersh, *My Lai 4,* pp. 128–43.
25. Army, *Peers Inquiry,* 1:2/12–2/13.
26. Hersh, *Cover-Up,* p. 251.
27. Army, *Peers Inquiry,* 1:12/34–12/35.

CHAPTER 2

1. Columbia Broadcasting System, "The Selling of the Pentagon," 23
   February 1971, and William J. Small, *Political Power and the Press*
   (New York: W.W. Norton, 1972), pp. 298–339.
2. Small, *Political Power,* pp. 311–74.
3. John M. Swomley, Jr., *Press Agents of the Pentagon* (Washington,
   D.C.: National Council against Conscription, July 1953).
4. C. Wright Mills, *The Power Elite* (New York: Oxford University
   Press, 1956), p. 220.
5. Samuel P. Huntington, *The Common Defense* (New York: Columbia University Press, 1961), pp. 384–88. Closer to the middle
   of the political spectrum were Morris Janowitz, *The Professional
   Soldier* (New York: Free Press, 1960), pp. 395–413; Gene M.
   Lyons, "PR and the Pentagon," *The New Leader,* 17 October

1960, pp. 10–12; Scott M. Cutlip and Allen H. Center, *Effective Public Relations,* 4th ed. (Englewood Cliffs, N.J.: 1971), pp. 607–33; Derek Shearer, "The Pentagon Propaganda Machine," in Leonard S. Rodberg and Derek Shearer, *The Pentagon Watchers* (Garden City, N.Y.: 1970), pp. 99–142; and Adam Yarmolinsky, *The Military Establishment* (New York: Harper and Row, 1971), pp. 194–210.

6. U.S., Congress, House, Committee on Armed Services, *Administration of the Service Academies, Report and Hearings of the Special Subcommittee on Service Academies.* 90th Cong., 1st and 2d sess., 1967–68, pp. 10927–28, 10948.

7. U.S., Congress, Senate, "Public Relations in the Department of Defense," 91st Cong., 2d sess., 1 December 1969, *Congressional Record,* pp. 15144–57; U.S., Congress, Senate, "Pentagon Propaganda," 91st Cong., 2d sess., 2 December 1969, *Congressional Record,* pp. 15306–33; U.S., Congress, Senate, "The Public Affairs Program of the Air Force," 91st Cong., 2d sess., *Congressional Record,* pp. 13649–74; U.S., Congress, Senate, "S.3217—A Bill Requiring the Secretary of Defense to Submit Regular Reports ...," 91st Cong., 2d sess., 5 December 1969, *Congressional Record,* pp. 15804–45.

8. The Comptroller General of the United States found that the "Department of Defense has been too conservative in defining its public affairs activities for purposes of reporting them." Indeed, while the Pentagon reported its total public affairs costs for fiscal year 1972 as amounting to $22.4 million, the GAO report cited expenditures for several activities it selected for review—special aerial teams, tours for distinguished civilians, operation of the Defense Information School, etc.—which alone would boost the Defense Department's figure by $24.5 million if included in the public affairs category. See U.S. Comptroller General, "Expenditures for Public Affairs Activities, Department of Defense," *Report to the Committee on Foreign Relations, United States Senate,* 30 July 1973.

9. J. William Fulbright, *The Pentagon Propaganda Machine* (New York: Liveright, 1970), pp. 25–27.

10. James L. McCamy, *Government Publicity* (Chicago: University of Chicago Press, 1939), pp. 222–25.

11. Joseph J. Mathews, *Reporting the Wars* (Minneapolis: University of Minnesota Press, 1957), pp. 12–51.

12. Cutlip and Center, *Effective Public Relations,* pp. 608–13. Much of the preceding paragraphs is based on this book.

13. Edwin Emery, *The Press and America* (Englewood Cliffs, N.J.: 1972), p. 513.

14. Cutlip and Center, *Effective Public Relations,* pp. 612–13.

15. Emery, *Press in America,* pp. 525–27.
16. C. W. Borklund, *The Department of Defense* (New York: Praeger, 1968), pp. 241–42.
17. Emery, *Press in America,* pp. 743–44.
18. Yarmolinsky, *Military Establishment,* p. 197.
19. Leo C. Rosten, *The Washington Correspondents* (New York: Harcourt, Brace, 1937), pp. 349–50.
20. Alfred Vagts, *A History of Militarism* (New York: Free Press, 1959), pp. 303–4.
21. James R. Wiggins, *Freedom or Secrecy* (New York: Oxford University Press, 1964), p. 94.
22. Frank Luther Mott, *American Journalism* (New York: Macmillan, 1961), pp. 99–101, 338.
23. Small, *Political Power,* p. 64.
24. Emery, *Press and America,* pp. 516–18; Mott, *American Journalism,* pp. 625–27; Small, *Political Power,* pp. 72–73.
25. Emery, *Press and America,* pp. 522–24. Although the Sedition Act was repealed in 1921, the Espionage and Trading with the Enemy acts were still in force. Even though their use this time was more judicious, they were used and at least indirectly continued to buttress the voluntary censorship program.
26. Mott, *American Journalism,* p. 627; Wiggins, *Freedom,* p. 96.
27. The Washington *Star,* 15 June 1973.
28. Wiggins, *Freedom,* p. 98.
29. Reprinted in ibid., pp. 98–99.
30. Emery, *Press in America,* p. 524.
31. Wiggins, *Freedom,* p. 100.
32. Carol M. Barker and Matthew H. Fox, *Classified Files: Yellowing Pages* (New York: Twentieth Century Fund, 1972), p. 12.
33. Ibid., pp. 15–16, pp. 19–24.
34. U.S., Congress, House, Foreign Operations and Government Information Subcommittee, *U.S. Government Information Policies and Practices—The Pentagon Papers (Part 2), Hearings,* 92nd Cong., 1st sess., 1971, p. 658.
35. U.S., Congress, House, Foreign Operations and Government Information Subcommittee, *U.S. Government Information Policies and Practices—The Pentagon Papers (Part 1), Hearings,* 92nd Cong., 1st sess., 1971, p. 12.
36. Ibid., p. 97.
37. U.S., Congress, House, Foreign Operations and Government Information Subcommittee, *U.S. Government Information Policies and Practices—Security Classification Problems Involving Subsection (b) (1) of the Freedom of Information Act, Hearings,* 92nd Cong., 2d sess., 1972, p. 2309.

38. Ibid., p. 2477.
39. Barker and Fox, *Classified Files*, p. 19.
40. Wiggins, *Freedom*, pp. 102–3.
41. Harry R. Ransom, *Can American Democracy Survive Cold War?* (Garden City, N.Y.: Doubleday, 1963), pp. 223–24.
42. Wiggins, *Freedom*, p. 109.
43. Ibid., p. 110.
44. William McGaffin and Erwin Knoll, *Anything But the Truth* (New York: Putnam's, 1969), pp. 66–67.
45. Arthur M. Schlesinger, Jr., *A Thousand Days* (Boston: Houghton Mifflin, 1965), pp. 260–61.
46. Clifton Daniel, "The Press and National Security," lecture to the World Press Institute, St. Paul, Minn., 1 June 1966, reprinted in ibid., pp. 197–208.
47. James Aronson, *The Press and the Cold War* (New York: Bobbs-Merrill, 1970), p. 162.
48. Quoted in Theodore F. Koop, *Weapon of Silence* (Chicago: University of Chicago Press, 1946), p. 163.
49. Reprinted in ibid., p. 265.
50. Wise, *Politics of Lying*, p. 138.
51. Pierre Salinger, *With Kennedy* (Garden City, N.Y.: Doubleday, 1966), p. 158.
52. Ransom, *Cold War*, p. 246.
53. Bruce Ladd, *Crisis in Credibility* (New York: New American Library, 1968), p. 149.
54. For one reporter's account, see McGaffin and Knoll, *Anything But the Truth*, pp. 209–12.
55. Small, *Political Power*, p. 198.
56. Ladd, *Crisis in Credibility*, pp. 145–46.
57. Arthur Sylvester, "The Government Has the Right to Lie," *Saturday Evening Post*, 19 November 1967, pp. 10–14.
58. Morley Safer, "Television Covers the War," in *Dateline 1966: Covering War* (New York: Overseas Press Club of America, 1966), p. 71.
59. Anonymous, "Secrecy: Review of Policies by Executive, Congress," *Congressional Quarterly*, 21 August 1971, p. 1785.
60. Robert O. Blanchard, "A History of the Federal Records Law," Freedom of Information Center Report no. 189 (Columbia, Mo.: University of Missouri School of Journalism, November 1967), pp. 1–12.
61. Kenneth Culp Davis, "The Information Act," *University of Chicago Law Review*, summer 1969, pp. 761–816; Joan M. Katz, "The Games Bureaucrats Play: Hide and Seek Under the Freedom of Information Act," *Texas Law Review* November 1970, pp. 1261–

84; K. D. Solomon, "The Freedom of Information Act: A Critical Review," *George Washington Law Review,* October 1969, pp. 150–63.

62. Harold C. Relyea, "Opening Government to Public Scrutiny: A Decade of Federal Efforts," *Public Administration Review* 35 (1975): 4.
63. What precisely is "bad" news? What is "negative" information? It is any information to which the public has a right but that Defense officials perceive as constituting a risk to themselves or the Pentagon. (That definition of risk draws on Louis P. Gawthrop, *Bureaucratic Behavior in the Executive Branch* [New York: Free Press, 1969]).

That leads to the next, more complex, question. To what information does the public have a right? To everything? If so, does that make for "workable democracy" in the administrative state? If not to everything, then only to that which Defense officials decide the public ought to know? But doesn't that imply a workable administrative state devoid of democracy?

The answers usually offered in response to those questions are not very helpful. They range from rather dogmatic assertions to descriptions of the "proper principles" involved. On one end of the spectrum the situation is seen as simple and stated bluntly: "Public business is the public's business. The people have the right to know." And that right is "subject only to those limitations imposed by the most urgent public necessity." (See Harold L. Cross, *The People's Right to Know* [Columbia University Press, 1953, p. xiii]. Unfortunately, what those limitations are is never spelled out in details precise enough to construct a useful operational definition. On the other end of the spectrum, the problem is seen as much more complex. Here the view is that a balance must be struck between the individual's right to privacy, the public's need for information about governmental affairs, and the "needs of government—the *raison d'état*"—to withhold information. (See Edward A. Shils, *The Torment of Secrecy* [Glencoe, Ill.: Free Press, 1956, pp. 21–27].) Francis E. Rourke has explored the secrecy-publicity-privacy triumvirate perhaps more carefully than anyone else, yet even he does not offer a clearcut definition of what information government needs to restrict and what information the public is entitled to know. (See his *Secrecy and Publicity* [Baltimore: Johns Hopkins Press, 1961]).

Consequently, this study relies on the Freedom of Information Act and the president's Executive Order 11652 on security classifications—which, together, spell out what material the federal government can withhold—to delimit to what information the public and, therefore, the media are entitled.

That has two advantages. First, the act and the executive order together strive to strike the balance Rourke and others see as necessary in a world where government has come to play a large part in every citizen's life, a world where destruction may only be 20 minutes away, but which still requires an informed citizenry if the democratic political system is to continue. Second, since the act and the order are now in force, the definition of unrestricted information they provide can be dismissed neither because it is too abstract nor because it is irrelevant to the "real world." On the contrary, they are binding on everyone working in the executive branch.

"Unrestricted information" then means any information about the Defense Department not specifically exempt from public disclosure either by being legitimately classified in accordance with Executive Order 11652 or by coming under one of the restrictive provisions of the Freedom of Information Act.

Finally, it should be made explicit that the concern here is only with the Defense Department's handling of unrestricted information requests from those wishing to publish it through the mass media. Consequently, the handling by the Pentagon of information requested by individuals for their private use, by defense contractors, by congressional committees, etc., is beyond the scope of this work.

64. Sidney H. Schanberg, "The Saigon Follies, or Trying to Head Them Off at 'Credibility Gap,' " *New York Times Magazine,* 12 November 1972, p. 39. See also, Wise, *Politics of Lying,* pp. 342–43; New York *Times,* 13 and 14 June 1972, Washington *Post,* 19 December 1972.

65. Morley Segal, "The Freedom of Information Act and Political Science Research," *PS* 2 (1969): 317.

66. Washington *Post,* 5 and 18 November 1971: Samuel J. Archibald, director, Washington office, Freedom of Information Center, University of Missouri, to G. Warren Nutter, assistant secretary of defense, international security affairs, 5 November 1971. Files, U.S., Congress, House, Subcommittee on Foreign Operations and Government Information.

67. Joseph C. Goulden, *Truth Is the First Casualty* (Chicago: Rand McNally, 1969), and Don Stillman, "Tonkin: What Should Have Been Asked?," *Columbia Journalism Review* 9 (winter 1970–71): 21–25.

68. J. Arthur Heise, *The Brass Factories* (Washington, D.C.: Public Affairs Press, 1969), pp. 4–5.

69. U.S., Congress, House, *Administration of the Service Academies,* pp. 10597–624.

70. New York *Times,* 13 June 1971; see also Hannah Arendt's analy-

sis, "Lying in Politics—Reflections on the the Pentagon Papers,"
in *Crises of the Republic* (New York: Harcourt Brace Jovanovich,
1972), pp. 3–47.
71. McGaffin and Knoll, *Anything But the Truth,* pp. 15–16; Ladd,
Crisis in Credibility, p. 136.

CHAPTER 3

1. U.S. Department of Defense, *Assistant Secretary of Defense,* directive no. 5122.5 (10 July 1961).
2. U.S. Department of Defense, *Clearance of Department of Defense
Public Information,* directive no. 5230.9 (24 December 1966), pp.
2–3.
3. U.S. Department of Defense, *Availability to the Public of Department of Defense Information,* directive no. 5400.7 (23 June 1967);
see also U.S. Department of Defense, office of the assistant secretary of defense for administration, *Availability of Information to the
Public,* administrative instruction no. 73 (14 August 1967).
4. U.S. Department of the Air Force, *Documentation—Disclosure of
Air Force Records,* air force regulation 12-30 (7 July 1970); U.S.
Department of the Army, *Release of Information to the Public,*
army regulation 340-17 (25 June 1973); U.S. Department of the
Navy, *Availability to the Public of the Navy Information and Records,* SECNAV instruction 5720.42A (6 January 1970).
5. Defense, *Availability to the Public of Department of Defense Information,* directive no. 5400.7 (14 February 1975); see also U.S.
Department of Defense, *Office of the Secretary of Defense/Organi-
zation of the Joint Chiefs of Staff Implementation of the DoD Freedom of Information Program,* directive no. 5400.10 (6 January
1976).
6. Phil G. Goulding, *Confirm or Deny* (New York: Harper and Row,
1970), p. 155.
7. Daniel Z. Henkin, "Statement before the Subcommittee on Department of Defense, Committee on Appropriations, U.S. Senate"
(May 1970), pp. 3–4.
8. The figures and those for the information directorate are for 1972.
See William E. Odom, executive assistant, office of the assistant
secretary of defense for public affairs, to Jerry W. Friedheim,
assistant secretary of defense for public affairs, 23 February 1973.
Files, assistant secretary of defense for public affairs, the Pentagon.
9. U.S. Department of the Army, office of the chief of information,
Standing Operating Procedures (1 July 1971); U.S. Department of
the Army, *Army Information General Policies,* army regulation

360-5 (27 September 1967); U.S. Department of the Navy, *Public Affairs Regulations,* SECNAV instruction 5720.44 (14 June 1974); U.S. Department of the Air Force, *Information Activities—Information Policies and Procedures,* air force manual 190-9 (22 September 1972).

10. Army regulation 360-5, pp. 5–6.
11. SECNAV instruction 5720.44, p. 3/2.
12. Army regulation 360-5, p. 8; Army, *Standing Operating Procedures,* p. 2/9; U.S. Department of the Army, office of the chief of information, *Functions—Office for the Freedom of Information* (November 1973), p. 1.
13. The New York *Times,* 5 January 1973.
14. U.S. Department of Defense, *Department of Defense Morning News Briefing* (by Deputy Assistant Secretary of Defense William Beecher), 12 June 1975, pp. 1–2.
15. U.S. Department of Defense, *Department of Defense Morning News Briefing* (by Deputy Assistant Secretary of Defense William Beecher), 30 April 1974, pp. 4–5.
16. Leon V. Sigal, *Reporters and Officials* (Lexington, Mass.: D. C. Heath, 1973), p. 104.
17. Ibid., pp. 111–15.
18. Ibid., p. 144.
19. The New York *Times,* 8 October 1973.
20. Seymour M. Hersh, "The Story Everyone Ignored," *Columbia Journalism Review* 8 (winter 1969–70): 55–58.
21. Joe Eszterhas, "The Toughest Reporter in America," *Rolling Stone,* 24 April 1975, p. 65.
22. Interviews with Fred Hoffman, Associated Press, 8 July 1974; Michael Getler, The Washington *Post,* 16 July 1974; and Capt. Ralph L. Slawson, Department of Defense, 2 July 1974, Washington, D.C.
23. See New York *Times,* 9 May 1974.

CHAPTER 4

1. Stephen Hartman, "The Impact of Defense Expenditures on the Domestic American Economy," *Public Administration Review* 33 (July/August 1973): 379–90.
2. Samuel P. Huntington, *The Common Defense* (New York: Columbia University Press, 1961), pp. 197–283, 384–404; Adam Yarmolinsky, *The Military Establishment* (New York: Harper and Row, 1971).

3. Bruce M. Russett, "Who Pays for Defense?," *The American Political Science Review* 63 (June 1969): 421.
4. E. E. Schattschneider, *The Semisovereign People* (New York: Holt, Rinehart and Winston, 1960), pp. 1–19.
5. Walter L. McMahon, "A Study of the Directorate for Security Review—Public Information Clearance Agency of the United States Department of Defense," Master's thesis, Pennsylvania State University, 1967, p. 272.
6. Ibid., pp. 271–76.
7. Ibid., p. 276.
8. Clark R. Mollenhoff, *The Pentagon* (New York: Pinnacle Books, 1967), p. 344.
9. McMahon, "A Study of the Directorate for Security Review," p. 278.
10. U.S., Congress, Senate, Special Preparedness Subcommittee of the Committee on Armed Services, *Military Cold War Education and Speech Review Policies.* S Rept., 87th Cong., 2d sess., 1962, p. 17.
11. McMahon, "A Study of the Directorate for Security Review," p. 278.
12. U.S. Department of Defense, Directorate for Security Review, *Indoctrination and Training Program, Training Block No. 4,* p. 3.
13. See, for example, Bertrand R. Canfield, *Public Relations* (Homewood, Ill.: Irwin, 1968), p. 358; Arthur Dreyer, "Military," in *Handbook for Public Relations* (New York: McGraw-Hill, 1971), pp. 225–27.
14. U.S. Department of Defense, *Responsibilities of the Office of Assistant Secretary of Defense (Public Affairs)—Functions of the Directorate for Security Review,* directive no. 5122.2 (17 August 1957; reprint with changes of 30 June 1961), p. 2.
15. U.S. Department of Defense, Directorate for Security Review, *Position Description—Director, Security Review* (undated), p. 1. See also U.S. Department of Defense, *Clearance of Department of Defense—Public Information,* directive no. 5230.9 (24 December 1966), pp. 2–3.
16. U.S. Department of the Army, *Army Information, General Practices,* army regulation 360-5 (27 September 1967), pp. 6–8; U.S. Department of the Army, *Army Information Officers' Guide,* army pamphlet no. 360-5 (August 1968), pp. 19/2–19/3.
17. U.S. Department of the Navy, *Public Affairs Regulations,* SECNAV INST 5720.44 (14 June 1974), pp. 4/1–4/2.
18. U.S. Department of the Air Force, *Information Activities—Review and Clearance of Department of the Air Force Information,* air force regulation 190-17 (4 February 1971), pp. 1–5; U.S. Depart-

ment of the Air Force, *Information Activities—Information Policies and Procedures,* air force manual 190-9 (22 September 1972), pp. 6/1–6/2.1.
19. Air force manual 190-9, p. 3/3, 3/8.
20. SECNAVINST 5720.44, p. 4/1, 4/3, 4/10.
21. Army pamphlet 360-5, p. 19/3, 19/2; army regulation 360-5, p. 6.
22. Interview with Charles W. Hinkle, director, Directorate for Security Review, 28 June 1974, Washington, D.C.
23. Charles W. Hinkle, director, security review, office of the assistant secretary of defense for public affairs, memorandum to the staff, "Review Responsibilities and General Procedures," 28 December 1962, p. 5.
24. Roger R. Bankson, director, defense information, and Charles W. Hinkle, director, security review, *Standing Operating Procedures Between the Directorate for Security Review and the Directorate for Defense Information, OASD(PA)* (3 May 1968), p. 1.
25. Defense, *Position Description—Director, Security Review,* p. 2.
26. U.S. Department of Defense, directorate of security review, *Position Description—Chief, OSD Division* (undated), p. 1.
27. Charles W. Hinkle, memorandum to the staff, p. 2.
28. Defense, *Position Description—Director, Security Review,* p. 1.
29. A. Ernest Fitzgerald, *The High Priests of Waste* (New York: W. W. Norton, 1972), pp. 85–92, 98.
30. C. Merton Tyrrell, *Pentagon Partners, The New Nobility* (New York: Grossman, 1970), pp. 3–4, 16–17, 19.
31. Milton C. Cummings, Jr., and David Wise, *Democracy under Pressure* (New York: Harcourt, Brace, Jovanovich, 1974), p. 401.
32. Phil G. Goulding, *Confirm or Deny* (New York: Harper and Row, 1970), pp. 25–49.
33. Ibid., pp. 49–51. See also John D. Williams, "Variables in Government/Media Interaction: Freedom of Information, Security and Social Responsibility," Ph.D. dissertation, University of Texas, 1972, pp. 95–110.
34. Quoted in David Wise, *The Politics of Lying* (New York: Random House, 1973), p. 11.
35. I. F. Stone, "Memo to the AP Editors: How Laird Lied," *New York Review of Books* 14 (4 June 1970), pp. 14–20.
36. Hannah Arendt, *Crisis of the Republic* (New York: Harcourt, Brace, and Jovanovich, 1972), p. 14.
37. Edwin Emery, *The Press and America* (Englewood Cliffs, N.J.: Prentice-Hall, 1972), p. 749.
38. The Washington *Star,* 15 June 1973.

CHAPTER 5

1. U.S., Congress, House, Foreign Operations and Government Information Subcommittee, *U.S. Government Information Policies and Practices—The Pentagon Papers,* (part 2), hearings, 92nd Cong., 1st sess., 1971, p. 391.
2. Ibid., part 4, p. 1242.
3. Francis E. Rourke, *Secrecy and Publicity* (Baltimore: Johns Hopkins Press, 1961), p. 38.
4. U.S., Congress, House, *U.S. Government Information Policies and Practices,* (part 7), pp. 2287–90.
5. For example, see U.S., Congress, House, *U.S. Government Information Policies and Practices,* (parts 1–7), passim; U.S., Congress, Senate, *Executive Privilege, Security in Government, Freedom of Information,* (vols. 1–3), Subcommittee on Intergovernmental Relations, Separations of Powers and Administrative Practice and Information, Hearings, 93rd Cong., 1st sess., passim.; David M. Wise, *The Politics of Lying* (New York: Random House, 1973).
6. U.S., Congress, House, *U.S. Government Information Policies and Practices,* (part 1), p. 99.
7. The Washington *Post,* 12 December 1971.
8. That is the definition of "top secret" in Executive Order 11652, "Classification and Declassification of National Security Information and Material," F.R. 5209, 10 March 1972.
9. James C. Goodale, ed., *The New York Times Company v. United States: A Documentary History* (New York: Arno Press, 1971), 1: 396–413.
10. Max Frankel, "The 'State Secrets" Myth," *Columbia Journalism Review* 10 (September-October 1971): 23–23.
11. For the experiences of other reporters and government officials, see Wise, *Politics of Lying,* pp. 89–133.
12. Frankel, "The 'State Secrets' Myth," pp. 23–26.
13. Statement reprinted in U.S., Congress, House, *U.S. Government Information Policies and Practices,* (part 7), p. 2844.
14. Reprinted in U.S., Congress, Senate, *Executive Privilege,* 1: 303, 304.
15. U.S. Department of the Army, office of the chief of information, *Standing Operating Procedures* (1 July 1971), p. 6/4 (as modified 17 November 1972).
16. U.S. Congress, House, *U.S. Government Information Policies and Practices,* Part 2, p. 393.
17. For instance, see Ibid., part 1, pp. 98–100, 226, 227.
18. Lloyd Shearer, "What Price Secrecy," *Parade,* August 22, 1971, p. 8; see also U.S., Congress, House, *U.S. Government Information*

Policies and Practices, part 2, p. 665, where Cooke indicates that the papers were designated "top secret" under derivative classification authority.

19. U.S., Congress, House, *U.S. Government Information Policies and Practices,* part 2, p. 753.
20. U.S., Congress, House, *U.S. Government Information Policies and Practices,* part 7, p. 2728.
21. Ibid., part 2, p. 666; part 7, p. 2729.
22. Wise, *Politics of Lying,* p. 60; Wise's report on the range of these superclassifications in use throughout the federal government is the best found publicly available; see pp. 55–87.
23. U.S. Department of Defense, *Availability to the Public of Department of Defense Information,* directive no. 5400.7 (14 February 1975), p. 3.
24. U.S. Department of the Air Force, *Information Activities—Information Programs and Procedures,* air force manual 190-9, 22 September 1972, p. 3/1.
25. U.S. Department of the Army, *Army Information Officers' Guide,* army pamphlet no. 260-5, August 1968, p. 19/2.
26. U.S. Department of the Navy, *Public Affairs Regulations,* SEC-NAV instruction 5720.44, 14 June 1974, p. 4/2.
27. U.S., Congress, House, *U.S. Government Information Policies and Practices,* part 2, pp. 667–68, 754.
28. Ibid., part 1, p. 103.
29. Ibid., part 7, p. 2727.
30. Ibid., part 5, pp. 1657–65.
31. Ibid., part 6, p. 2122, 2135.
32. Interviews with Robert L. Gilliat, office of the general counsel, Dept. of Defense, 12 December 1973; James L. Nash, chief, records management branch, office of the secretary of defense, 3 July 1974; and Charles Hinkle, director, Security and Policy Review, 27 and 28 June 1974, all in Washington, D.C.
33. Interviews with Lou Arrants, William Donohoe, and Reinhold Herman, Office for the Freedom of Information, office of secretary of the army, 19 June 1974; Lt. Col. Leonard F. B. Reed, Jr., Office of the Chief of Information, Dept. of the Army, 24 June and 9 July 1974; Bland West and Capt. Ronald E. Stouffer, office of the general counsel, office of the secretary of the army, 20 June 1974, all in Washington, D.C.
34. Interviews with Saul Katz, office of the general counsel, Department of the Navy, 10 July 1974; Daniel Dinan, Isaac Manuel, and Richard Welsh, Office of Naval Intelligence, 26 June 1974; and Ronald R. Kay, Michael L. George, Donald G. Smith, judge advo-

cate general's Office, Department of the Navy, 10 July 1974, all in
Alexandria, Virginia.

35. Interviews with Capt. David M. Johnson, office of the general
Counsel, Department of the Air Force, 29 June 1974, and Col.
John J. Pelszynski, chief, Office of Security Review, Office of Information, Department of the Air Force, 21 June 1974, all in Washington.

36. U.S. Department of Defense, directive no. 5400.7 (23 June 1967);
U.S. Department of the Air Force, *Documentation—Disclosure of
Air Force Records,* air force regulation 12-30 (7 July 1970); U.S.
Department of the Army, *Release of Information to the Public,*
army regulation 340-17 (25 June 1973); U.S. Department of the
Navy, *Availability to the Public of Department of Navy Information
and Records,* SECNAV instruction 5720.42 A (6 January 1970).

37. U.S., Congress, House, *U.S. Government Information Policies and
Practices,* part 2, pp. 390–778; part 6, pp. 2101–44; part 8, pp.
3186–96, and U.S., Congress, Senate, *Executive Privilege,* part 2,
pp. 81–95.

38. U.S., Congress, Senate, *Executive Privilege,* 1: 157–67. (See also the
New York *Times,* 22 November 1972, 20 January 1973.) The
Associated Press made a similar series of requests for documents
classified at least 10 years ago. Of eight requests the AP had made
since June 1, 1972, seven had not produced the desired material by
December of that year. The one exception turned out to have been
a document previously declassified. In the case of some Korean
War documents, the AP was told that a search would require "an
unreasonable amount of effort." After the AP pointed out that
President Eisenhower had referred to the material in his memoirs,
Pentagon officials said they would search further. See the Washington *Post,* 1 December 1972.

39. U.S., Congress, Senate, *Executive Privilege,* 2: 197.

40. Jack H. Taylor to J. Arthur Heise, 30 November 1974.

41. For example, see Jack H. Taylor to Lt. Col. Leonard F. B. Reed,
chief, news branch, office of the chief of information, U.S. army,
8 December 1972, 2 January 1973 (files, U.S., Congress, House,
Subcommittee on Foreign Operations and Government Information).

42. Reed to Charles L. Bennett, managing editor, *The Daily Oklaho-
man-Oklahoma City Times,* 10 April, 16 April 1973.

43. Taylor to Rep. William S. Moorhead, chairman, U.S., Congress,
House, Subcommittee on Foreign Operations and Government
Information.

44. Taylor to Reed, 15 January 1973.

45. U.S. Department of the Navy, "Report of the Study of the Navy's

Public Affairs Program and Future Requirements," by Vice Admiral William P. Mack, Rear Admiral John J. Shanahan, Captain Oliver L. Norman, Captain David B. Cooney, and Captain Larry J. Brown (Washington, D.C., 1973), p. 33.
46. Hanson H. Baldwin, "Managed News—Our Peacetime Censorship," *Atlantic,* April 1963, p. 54.
47. Jules Witcover, "The Surliest Crew in Washington," *Columbia Review* 4 (spring 1965): 12.
48. Richard Fryklund, "Covering the Defense Establishment," in Ray E. Hiebert, ed., *The Press in Washington* (New York: Dodd, Mead, 1966), p. 167.
49. The Washington *Examiner,* 11–13 December, 1969.
50. Wise, *The Politics of Lying,* p. 239.

CHAPTER 6

1. U.S. Department of the Army, *Army Information, General Policies,* army regulation 360–5 (27 September 1967), p. 3.
2. U.S. Department of the Air Force, *Information Activities—Information Policies and Procedures,* air force manual 190–9 (22 September 1972), p. 3/1.
3. U.S. Department of the Navy, Public Affairs Regulations, SECNAVINST 5720.44 (14 June 1974), p. 1/1.
4. U.S. Department of Defense, *Dictionary of Military and Associated Terms* (Washington: Joint Chiefs of Staff, 3 January 1972), p. 240.
5. Army regulations 360–5, p. 2.
6. Air force manual 190–0, p. 1/1.
7. Navy, SECNAVINST 5720.44, p. 1/2.
8. U.S. Department of the Navy, "Report of the Study of the Navy's Public Affairs Program and Future Requirements," by Vice Admiral William P. Mack, Rear Admiral John J. Shanahan, Captain Larry J. Brown (Washington, D.C., 1973), p. 83.
9. Robert H. Ziegler, information specialist, Defense Information School, to J. Arthur Heise, 31 October 1974. In addition to the active-duty military personnel, reserve enlisted and officer personnel also attend the school for abbreviated courses. A number of civil service employees also attend annually.
10. Richard A. Sones, "An Analytical Study of Army Information Officer Problems and Training," master's thesis, Texas Tech University, 1972, p. 47.
11. U.S. Department of Defense, Defense Information School, Public Affairs Department, *Handbook* (1972), inside front cover, pp. 1/3, 2/1, 2/11, 3/1, 3/11, 7/11 and 12/1.

12. Sones, "An Analytical Study," pp. 60–62. The 156 officers to whom Sones sent the questionnaire constitute one-half of the army's authorized information officer positions at the time. Sixty-six percent responded. Among the 156 were 46 DINFOS officer graduates. Sones does not indicate how their responses, if at all, differed from the non-DINFOS officers.
13. U.S. Department of the Army, ". . . memo used in modified form in 1947 . . . to brief Gen. Dwight Eisenhower, to sell him on peacetime P.R. function."
14. Frances E. Rourke, *Secrecy and Publicity* (Baltimore: Johns Hopkins Press, 1961), pp. 36–37.
15. Army regulation 360–5, p. 5.
16. U.S. Department of the Army, office of the chief of information, *Standing Operating Procedures* (1 July 1971), p. 1/18.
17. Navy, SECNAVINST 5720.44, p. 4/14.
18. Navy, Office of Information, *Standard Operating Procedures* (27 September 1973), pp. 7–8.
19. Air force manual 190–9, p. 3/3.
20. Air force manual 190–9, p. 3/3.
21. Army regulation 360–5, p. 8.
22. Navy, SECNAVINST 5720.44, p. 4/18.
23. Navy, *Report of the Study,* p. 33.
24. Brig. Gen. Joseph F. H. Cutrona, director, Defense Information, memorandum for the assistant secretary of defense (public affairs), "Weekly Activities Report—Directorate of Defense Information," 7 December 1973.
25. The New York *Times,* 7 June, 12 September 1973.
26. U.S. Department of Defense, *Delineation of DoD Audio-Visual Public Affairs Responsibilities and Policies,* Department of Defense instruction 5410.15 (3 November 1966), pp. 1–4.
27. *Procedures for DoD Assistance on Production of Non-Government Motion Pictures and Television Programs,* Department of Defense instruction 5410.16 (21 January 1964), pp. 1–4.
28. Russell E. Shain, "Effects of Pentagon Influence on War Movies, 1948–70," *Journalism Quarterly* 49 (winter 1972): 647.
29. Army regulation 360–5 (27 September 1967), pp. 10–13, plus change no. 3 (21 November 1973). For the navy and air force, see SECNAVINST 5720.44, pp. 4/15–4/17 and air force manual 190–9, pp. 3/10–3/14.
30. U.S. Department of Defense, Defense Information School, *Handbook,* p. 7/2; army regulations 360.5, change no. 2 (20 October 1971), pp. 1–2; Navy, SECNAVINST 5720.44, 4/3; air force manual 190–9, pp. 2/5–3/6.

CHAPTER 7

1. It should be noted, perhaps, that it is not peculiar for the military profession to adhere to a specific set of norms and values. Other professions also have their ideologies (see Herbert Kaufman, *The Forest Ranger* [Baltimore: Johns Hopkins University Press, 1960].
2. Samuel P. Huntington, *The Soldier and the State* (Cambridge, Mass.: Harvard University Press, 1957), pp. 19–58.
3. See Bengt Abrahamsson, *Military Professionalization and Political Power* (Stockholm: Goetebargs Offsettryckeri, 1971), pp. 76–79.
4. Huntington, *Soldier and the State,* pp. 62–63, 90.
5. This question is based on the fact that omissions and distortions do occur as information flows through complex organizations. Perhaps the best empirically based overview of the problems of organizational communication is Harold Guetzkow, "Communications in Organizations," in James G. March, ed., *Handbook of Organizations* (Chicago: Rand McNally, 1965), pp. 534–73. See also Peter M. Blau and Richard W. Scott, *Formal Organizations* (San Francisco: Chandler, 1962), pp. 22–58; James G. March and Herbert A. Simon, *Organizations* (New York: Wiley 1958), pp. 161–69; William Parsons and Don L. Bowen, *Communication in Public Administration* (University, Ala.: Bureau of Public Administration, University of Alabama, 1965), pp. 11–37, 49–65; Herbert A. Simon, *Administrative Behavior* (New York: Free Press, 1957), pp. 154–71; Herbert A. Simon, Donald W. Smithburg, and Victor A. Thompson, *Public Administration* (New York: Knopf, 1950), pp. 218–43; Lee Thayer, "Communication and Organization Theory," in Frank E. X. Dance, ed., *Human Communication Theory* (New York: Holt, Rinehart and Winston, 1967), pp. 70–117; Harold Wilensky, *Organizational Intelligence* (New York: Basic Books, 1967), pp. 41–74. For one former insider's personal observations, see Charles Frankel, *High on Foggy Bottom* (New York: Harper and Row, 1969), pp. 78–93.

However, these internal communications problems can be overemphasized. Obviously, as long as an organization functions, it is overcoming information pathologies at least to the minimum degree necessary, doing so primarily by building redundancy into its communication network and by relying on more than one feedback loop between superior and subordinate levels in the hierarchy as well as between units on the same level. As a recent study by Herbert Kaufman and Michael Couzens indicates, public bureaucracies thereby also overcome these information problems. See their *Administrative Feedback* (Washington, D.C.: Brookings Institution, 1973), p. 63.

6. Regulations and manuals governing the information programs in the three services reflect these feedback loops. The navy's chief of information, for example, is one of the recipients of reports made over a navy-wide "special incident reporting system." In addition, public affairs officers in the area where such incidents occur are also warned to maintain liaison with the navy's information office in the Pentagon. (See U.S. Department of the Navy, *Public Affairs Regulations,* SECNAVINST 5720.44, 14 June 1974, p. 4/4.) Army information officers are similarly instructed to stay in touch with higher and lower levels of their service. Indeed, in case of doubt about whether information is releasable, IOs below the level of the army's headquarters in Washington are encouraged to contact either the next higher headquarters or the top level of the army in the Pentagon. Furthermore, the army chief of information "is authorized direct communication with information officers at all levels." (See *Army Information Officers' Guide,* army pamphlet No. 360–5, August 1968, p. 2/2.) Similarly, air force information officers "at all levels are authorized to communicate directly on information matters" with any necessary level of their service. Further, each IO is to immediately inform the air force information office in the Pentagon "of any incident or event that is likely to be of immediate national news interest, or of any conditions that might cause an undesirable reaction or unfavorable publicity for the Air Force." (See *Information Activities—USAF Information Program,* air force regulation 190–41, 12 June 1973, p. 5.)

7. Phil G. Goulding, *Confirm or Deny* (New York: Harper and Row, 1970).

8. U.S. Department of the Army, office of the chief of information, *Functions—Office for the Freedom of Information* (November 1973), p. 1.

9. U.S. Department of the Navy, "Report of the Study of the Navy's Public Affairs Program and Future Requirements," by Vice Admiral William P. Mack, Rear Admiral John J. Shanahan, Captain Oliver L. Norman, Captain David B. Cooney, and Captain Larry J. Brown (Washington, D.C., 1973), pp. 102–18; interviews with Cmdr. Jack M. White, director, program planning, Office of Information, U.S. navy, Washington, D.C., 26 June 1974, and Capt. David B. Cooney, deputy chief of information, U.S. navy, Washington, D.C., 25 June 1974.

10. Interviews with Lt. Col. C. B. Kelly III, chief, Operations Forces Branch, Office of Information, U.S. air force, Washington, D.C., 27 June 1974, and Mark H. Gilman, assistant director for operations, Office of Information, U.S. air force, Washington, D.C., 24 June 1974. See also U.S. Department of the Navy, *Report of the Study,* pp. 116–17.

11. U.S. Department of the Air Force, air force regulation 190–41.
12. Interview with Lt. Col. Burton A. Eddy, deputy chief, Administrative and Management Division, Office of Information, U.S. army, 24 June 1974, Washington, D.C.
13. Richard A. Sones, "An Analytical Study of Army Information Officer Problems and Training" master's thesis, Texas Tech University, 1972, p. 80, 83–86.
14. Ibid., p. 103.
15. Navy, "Biography of Rear Admiral William Thompson."
16. Navy, "Biography of Capt. David M. Cooney."
17. Army, "Biography of Maj. Gen. L. Gordon Hill, Jr."
18. Army, "Biography of Brig. Gen. James A. Herbert."
19. Air Force, "Biography of Maj. Gen. Guy E. Hairston, Jr."
20. Air Force, "Biography of Brig. Gen. James R. Brickel."
21. Army, Office for the Freedom of Information, "Types of Army FoI Conferences—Panel Participation Exercises" (27 June 1974).
22. Hanson W. Baldwin, "The Information War in Saigon," *The Reporter,* 24 February 1966, pp. 29–31.
23. The New York *Times,* 12 June 1971.
24. U.S. Department of Defense, *Availability to the Public of Defense Department Information,* directive no. 5400.7 (23 June 1967), p. 19.
25. John D. Williams, "Variables in Government/Media Interaction: Freedom of Information, Security, and Social Responsibility," Ph.D. dissertation, University of Texas, 1972, pp. 214–15.
26. A. M. Rosenthal, "The Iconoclastic Age," (text of speech, edited from transcript, given at the Naval War College, November 1973).
27. David Halberstam, "In Search of Trust and Confidence" (text of speech, edited from transcript, given at the Naval War College, November 1973), p. 5.
28. Stansfield Turner, closing remarks, Military-Media Conference (18 November 1972).
29. Jack M. White, "The Military and the Media," *U.S. Naval Institute Proceedings,* July 1974, pp. 48–49.
30. Interviews with Capt. David M. Cooney, Cmdr. Jack M. White.
31. Cmdr. Jack M. White, director, Program Planning Division, Office of Information, U.S. navy, to deputy chief of information, U.S. navy, 28 February 1974.
32. *Confirm or Deny,* p.46.
33. Lt. Col. Sanford H. Winston, Directorate for Plans and Programs, office of the assistant secretary of defense for public affairs, to Arthur Sylvester, assistant secretary of defense for public affairs, office of the secretary of defense, 19 April 1964.

CHAPTER 8

1. Leon V. Sigal, *Reporters and Officials* (Lexington, Mass.: D. C. Heath, 1973), pp. 80–81.
2. Lester Markel, "The 'Management' of News," *Saturday Review,* 9 February 1963, p. 50 and p. 61.
3. Gay Talese, *The Kingdom and the Power* (New York: World Publishing Co., 1969), pp. 445–51.
4. Phil G. Goulding, *Confirm or Deny* (New York: Harper and Row, 1970), pp. 79–81.
5. Seymour M. Hersh, "From the Pentagon—(But Don't Tell Anyone I Told You)," *The New Republic,* 19 December 1967, pp. 13–14.
6. Derek Shearer, "The Brass Image," *The Nation,* 20 April 1970, p. 463.
7. Jules Witcover, "Where Washington Correspondents Failed," *Columbia Journalism Review* 8 (winter 1970–71): 8, 9. That assessment represented a reversal of Witcover's views of the newsmen covering the Pentagon. In the mid-1960s, he had written another article for the same journal, entitled, "The Surliest Crew in Washington," and subtitled: "The two dozen correspondents who spend their working lives in the Pentagon trust no one, including each other. Here is how they practice their specialties: baiting the brass, outflanking the information officers, and nursing suspicions." See Jules Witcover, "The Surliest Crew in Washington," *Columbia Journalism Review* 5 (spring 1965): 11.
8. Neil Sheehan, *The Arnheiter Affair* (New York: Random House, 1971), p. 266.
9. Clark R. Mollenhoff, *The Pentagon* (New York: Pinnacle Books, 1972), pp. 398, 521.
10. Adam Yarmolinsky, *The Military Establishment* (New York: Harper and Row, 1971), p. 214–15.
11. Brit Hume and Mark McIntyre, "Polishing Up the Brass," *More,* June 1973, p. 7.
12. Sigal, *Reporters and Officials,* p. 128.
13. William L. Rivers, *The Adversaries* (Boston: Beacon Press, 1970).
14. Douglass Cater, *The Fourth Branch of Government* (Boston: Houghton Mifflin, 1959).
15. Alan A. Altshuler, ed., *The Politics of the Federal Bureaucracy* (New York: Dodd, Mead, 1968), p. 381.
16. Edward A. Shils, *Torment of Secrecy,* (Glencoe, Ill.: Free Press, 1956), pp. 37–38.
17. Francis E. Rourke, *Secrecy and Publicity,* (Baltimore: Johns Hopkins Press, 1961), p. 188.

18. Aronson, *The Press and the Cold War;* Aronson, *Deadline for the Media* (Indianapolis: Bobbs-Merrill, 1972); Ben Bagdikian, *The Effete Conspiracy* (New York: Harper and Row, 1972).
19. Dan D. Nimmo, *Newsgathering in Washington* (New York: Atherton Press, 1964), p. 227.
20. Talese, *The Kingdom and the Power,* p. 339.
21. Witcover, "Surliest Crew," p. 12.
22. John D. Williams, "Variables in Government/Media Interaction: Freedom of Information, Security and Social Responsibility," Ph.D. dissertation, University of Texas, 1972, pp. 197–98, 202, 233–34.

CHAPTER 9

1. Kurt Lang, *Military Institutions and the Sociology of War* (Beverly Hills, Calif.: Sage, 1972), pp. 58–66.
2. As the former head of the press relations section of the United States Information Service in Vietnam and later vice-president of Time, Inc., put it: "One of the headaches we used to face in Vietnam was that too many of our press officers, both military and civilian, had been plucked out of post PAO jobs where they had been involved really only in publicity (they knew the story they were writing was going to get into that post newspaper) and plunked down in the middle of the hottest, most controversial, most complex story in the world today and asked to do a real information job, a press job." See Barry Zorthian, "Effective Press Relations," *Marine Corps Gazette,* June 1970, p. 14.
3. U.S., Congress, House, Foreign Operations and Government Information Subcommittee, *U.S. Government Information Policies and Practices,* part 6, 92nd Cong., 2d sess., 1972, p. 2244.

Index